Sharpening Your **People** skills

Sharpening Your **People** skills

10 Tools for success in any Relationship

WILLIAM J. DIEHM

BROADMAN
&HOLMAN
PUBLISHERS

Nashville, Tennessee

4262-88
0-8054-6288-0

Published by Broadman & Holman Publishers
Nashville, Tennessee
Acquisitions & Development Editor, Vicki Crumpton
Interior Design by Leslie Joslin

Dewey Decimal Classification: 158
Subject Heading: HUMAN RELATIONS / APPLIED
PSYCHOLOGY / CHRISTIAN LIFE
Library of Congress Card Catalog Number: 96-11432

Unless otherwise noted, Scripture quotations are from the King James Version of the Bible. Other passages are NIV, the Holy Bible New International Version, copyright © 1973, 1978, 1984 by International Bible Society; and NKJV, New King James Version, copyright © 1979, 1980, 1982, Thomas Nelson, Inc., Publishers.

Library of Congress Cataloging-in-Publication Data
Diehm, William J.
     Sharpening your people skills : ten tools for success in any relationship / William J. Diehm.
        p. cm.
    ISBN 0-8054-6288-0 (pbk.)
    1. Interpersonal communication. 2. Interpersonal communication—Religious aspects—Christianity. 3. Interpersonal relations. 4. Interpersonal relations—Religious aspects—Christianity. 5. Invective. I. Title.
BF637.C45D52   1996
158.2—dc20
                               96-11432
                                 CIP

96 97 98 99 00 5 4 3 2 1

CONTENTS

INTRODUCTION

When I was a little boy of nine, in the good old summertime, the nice lady across the street from our home in Pasco, Washington, invited my mother and me to a chicken dinner. We were in the midst of the Great Depression, and chicken dinners were rare in those days. When we arrived at her home, it was obvious that Mrs. Mueller had worked hard all day to make a sumptuous feast.

I was wolfing down mashed potatoes and gravy, and I had tasted a piece of fried chicken when Mrs. Mueller asked me, "Billy, how do you like the chicken?"

I did not respond so she repeated, "Billy, how do you like the chicken?"

I still said nothing, and my mother chided me, "Billy, answer Mrs. Mueller."

"Do I have to tell the truth, Ma?"

"Of course, Son. I have always taught you to tell the truth."

"Well, OK," I answered. "It tastes like chicken manure."

"Billy!" my mother shouted. I don't remember the rest of the meal, but when I got home my mother said, "Billy, why did you hurt Mrs. Mueller's feelings like that?"

"Mom, you always told me to tell the truth, and it did taste like chicken manure to me."

Maybe Mrs. Mueller had broken the gall while cleaning the chicken. Maybe I had defective taste buds. Who knows? One thing is clear: I had tried to be scrupulously honest, and I had severely hurt the feelings of a well-meaning neighbor. As a young child, my people skills were immature, and it is fairly obvious that blunt negative truth is not the way to win friends and influence people.

Recently, a charming, intelligent, and personable acquisitions editor from Broadman & Holman (notice my people skills) asked me to consider writing a book on people skills. She said, "You are certainly qualified to do so." I suppose she meant that I was a former pastor, psychologist, and teacher of the Dale Carnegie Courses. What really qualifies me to write such a book as *Sharpening Your People Skills* is the innumerable stupid mistakes I have made. Thomas Edison replied to the question, "What have you been doing?" by saying, "I have learned 2,000 ways how not to make an electric light." I have learned hundreds of ways how not to handle people.

Over the years, I have confronted the dilemma of truth versus tact, particularly when people put me on the spot with leading questions such as "You don't remember my name, do you?" No, sometimes I don't remember their names, but I am reluctant to say so.

One day I played a trombone solo at church. I asked a friend, Earl Atterberry, how he liked it. He replied, "Don't ask, if you don't want to know."

I have learned to protect myself from hurt by not asking leading questions that require people to tell "white lies." It is a little more difficult, however, when people back you into a corner and force you into a white lie.

I am hoping that *Sharpening Your People Skills* will help us to deal with people in such a way that we can tell the truth in love and avoid as much hurt as possible. Hopefully, reading and studying and practicing people skills will enable a person to be tactful without losing honesty. Bearings make wheels turn smoothly, but without a little grease the wheels vociferously howl and quickly break down. People skills are the grease that makes relationships wheel smoothly.

PART I

SHARPENING YOUR PEOPLE SKILLS

CHAPTER 1

BENEFITS OF PEOPLE SKILLS

"All things whatsoever ye would that men should do to you, do ye even so to them."

—JESUS, MATTHEW 7:12

- Do you find yourself getting in trouble for the same thing over and over again?
- Do people often say to you, "You'll never change."
- Do you think that people are too sensitive and are always getting their feelings hurt?
- Do you often find yourself saying, "Can't you take a joke?" or "I was just joking"?
- Have you been told that you are tactless or tasteless, and have you come to be a little proud of it?
- Honestly, do you get along well with people?

Why should we be nice to people? They aren't always nice to us. Perhaps we are wonderful, Christlike people who are being persecuted for righteousness' sake. More than likely, however, we are being persecuted for our own stupidity and lack of tact. Perhaps people aren't nice to us because we violate the rules of interpersonal relationships, or maybe we haven't taken the time to learn people skills. In his classes, Dale Carnegie often said, "We spend more time studying the mating habits of the bullfrog than in learning how to get along with people."

Dealing effectively with people can be complex and fraught with failure, but it helps the situation to understand the culture of people, to learn how to accept and love them, and to try to treat them as we want to be treated.

We can be motivated to learn how to manage interpersonal relationships when we realize that life will go more smoothly, we will earn the respect of others, people will befriend us, we may make more money, we will be healthier, we will have fewer enemies, we will be happier, life will be more pleasant and livable to the people around us—and the greatest reason of all: God will smile on our relationships.

LIFE WILL GO MORE SMOOTHLY

Some people apparently take perverse pleasure in upsetting, dividing, and estranging fellow passengers on the journey of life. These abrasive people love to be embroiled in an imbroglio. They are hot to trot to a brouhaha where they can create a free-for-all. They are constantly suggesting that you and someone else have a rhubarb while they watch. Whenever these combative ones come into a room, they throw around the spirit of contention through the skillful use of evil innuendo. These destructive devils often hide behind a smile, hypocritical faith, pacemaking, or beguiling innocence as they make false accusations or spread malicious slander to divide friends, families, churches, communities, or even nations. It would pay such people to get motivated to learn people skills, and it would pay us ordinary people to learn how to get along with the difficult ones, if possible. When we learn people skills, we make life a little easier for everyone.

People who are not motivated to get along with others soon discover that others do not want to get along with them.

Jack Kennedy once said on TV about two supporters who couldn't get along, "If they don't make peace, they will bring my program down." When people can't get along there is little opportunity for Kingdom building.

A long time ago Jesus prayed that His disciples would be one, even as He and His Father were one, that the world might believe that God sent Him. So many followers of Jesus have difficulty getting along with each other that it is little wonder why the whole world has not been converted.

People skills are the grease in the wheels of human relationships. Learning how to deal with people is a discipline that is as demanding as learning how to play the piano, and perhaps no other skill in the world can make life more pleasant than applying ourselves to it.

WE EARN THE RESPECT OF OTHERS

The wimpy people, who like Anthony Eaton of World War II fame want "peace at any price," are as bad as the fighters. They will compromise and kowtow to anyone, even Adolf Hitler. The wimps don't know that no one likes or respects a person who stands for nothing. The more one ingratiates himself, the less he is respected. Jesus wisely said, "Woe to you when all men speak well of you" (Luke 6:26, NIV). Undoubtedly that person has made a wimpy attempt to be liked by all, giving up all his principles to try to please everyone—yet he pleases no one.

To me, one of our great presidents was Jimmy Carter, a man of honor and integrity, a Sunday school teacher, a man who kept his word. Jimmy Carter fell into disrepute with some of the American people and failed to be reelected president. Why? He was everything a president could possibly be. According to the media, he lost status because he did not take a stronger stand in the Iranian crisis when they captured our embassy and held Americans hostage. Of course, President Carter was trying to save the lives of our people, which he did, but in the process he acquired the reputation of being a weak president. My editor told me of two surveys that asked the question, "Which star would you want as president?" In each survey, Clint Eastwood was number one. We seem to want tough and violent men to lead us.

I remember one time when my father sent me out to chop some wood for our old kitchen range. In a malicious, angry way, I proceeded to chop up the wood box. My father slipped up behind me, tapped me on the shoulder, and, when I turned my head, he slapped me on the face. I have never forgotten that day when I developed some character. Not only have I not chopped up any more wood bins, but I still love and respect my father for taking a firm position.

Getting along with people is a delicate balancing act between permissiveness and firmness. If you are a wimp, people will walk on you and hate you for it; and if you are always fighting with people, they can't stand that either.

In my book *Finding Your Life Partner*, I recall the time when I told my high school-aged daughter that she could not go to a public dance with a blind date. I found her later in her room crying. "Carolyn," I exclaimed, "I did this for your own safety." She responded, "I don't mind not going, Daddy. I'm crying because now I know that you love me when you won't let me go to a place like that." Today, that principle is called "tough love." It also might be called "true love" because it is the only kind of love that creates respect.

The book *How to Win Friends and Influence People* by Dale Carnegie was a classic in its day. One of the main ideas of the book is to find something good about people and call that to their attention—a wonderful idea. In these evil days, though, it is also important to admonish and correct if we want others' respect.

Certainly, we are not to make war for the love of war, nor are we to make peace at the price of principles. We are under the admonition that God is love, and we are called to love our neighbor as ourselves. In the name of love, God requires that we shape up; so when we love our neighbor, we must require that he or she shapes up too. Effectively dealing with people demands both compassion and firmness of principle. When we develop people skills, we neither compromise our standards nor make unrelenting war. Rather, we try to make a just peace.

PEOPLE WILL BEFRIEND US

If there is no other motivation or reason for developing people skills, then let it be known, if you want people to befriend you and give you a break, you must befriend them and give them a break. It makes good movie drama to watch a tough boss chewing out his workers, but in real life the boss is likely to get sued. A boss or leader inspires, challenges, and encourages his employees. Children love tough teachers who are fair and kind, but they avoid those who have the reputation of being cranky and unfriendly. We expect our politicians to be honest and also friendly. The friendly man gets the votes. Salespersons who are friendly often make the sale. Doctors with good bedside manners more easily gain the trust and confidence of their patients, speeding the healing process.

As long as I live, I will never forget the time a friend severely reprimanded an employee for incompetence and flagrant disregard of his company policies. The employee took revenge—he went home and committed suicide. What anguish it brought to my friend's soul—his hard line had backfired. The employee's wife filed strong protestations and berated my friend for his lack of sensitivity. It cost my friend his job, and rightly so; there are many more positive ways of dealing with incompetent employees. The tough-guy, hardline confrontation is dangerous. To manage his employees and keep his job, my friend sorely needed people skills.

Many people are awkward and clumsy in dealing with others. They are constantly saying and doing things that violate the culturally acceptable way of behaving. We need to learn how to deal with people, and we need to be certain that we have not become one of the awkward ones.

How do people make it in this world without friends? The answer is simple: they don't. How do we make friends? Again the answer is relatively simple: we must pay attention to the wants, needs, culture, and personalities of people. In short, we must develop people skills to have friends.

Every year at Christmastime I send out a newsletter to all my friends. One year I received a note from a long-time friend, who wrote, "Bill, after all these years, don't you have anything to say to me personally except a copy of your stupid form letter?"

I was momentarily offended, and then I thought, *He's right. I was actually informing him that I was too busy to give him the personal attention that friendship demands.*

WE MAY MAKE MORE MONEY

Money is not a popular subject in the Christian world. Somehow we have been conditioned to believe that making money is inherently evil. Jesus said that the rich would have a difficult time getting into the kingdom of heaven, and those who trust in riches instead of God won't make it. But Jesus also urged us to be good stewards of our money. Remember, a rich man provided the grave for the body of our Lord. Making money is OK as long as our faith is not in money but in God, and we are generous and giving. Making lots of money and having good people skills are not correlated on a one-to-one basis. However, money comes from people, and knowing how to deal with people is a good money-making skill. Corporations hire people not to make enemies, but to influence people in a positive way.

My friend Gene Hall works for a large mobile home builder who puts ready-made houses on lots all over the country. Outside of his occupation he works with youth in sports programs and in the church. I asked him, "How does this fit in with your business?" He replied, "I make friends, and without friends you cannot sell mobile homes, and without sales the whole business grinds to a halt." When he makes friends, he makes money.

One of the surest ways to have enough is to give enough. The principle "Give and it shall be given unto you" is true. Service, or giving to people, is one of the basic premises of people skills. Have you ever asked the question, "How did that person get to be my friend?" Think about it. That person probably remembered your birthday or anniversary. He or she was constantly doing little things and expressing little loyalties that pulled him or her into the circle of your life. The giving person has friends and friends take care of friends.

There is a biblical story of a wise steward who made friends with his master's debtors before the master fired him. He was wise—he knew he needed friends to get support and make money. Jesus closes this story by saying, "I tell you, use worldly wealth to gain friends for yourselves, so that when it is gone, you will be welcomed into eternal dwellings" (Luke 16:9, NIV).

There is no absolute guarantee that the development of people skills will make money, but we can be sure that bad people skills will keep us poor.

WE WILL BE HEALTHIER

When Richard Nixon was president of the United States, he was indicted for alleged crimes in an event called "Watergate." He resigned from the presidency, and shortly after that President Gerald Ford gave him a full pardon. During the interim between his resignation and the pardon, ex-President Nixon almost died from phlebitis. Was that a coincidence? No! Physical illness often follows stressful situations.

One of the great problems in today's health world is the condition of depression, and one of the chief contributors to depression is stress. Stress often grows from bad relationships with people. So if we want to keep well, we must keep up on the psychology of coping with the crowd.

Psychosomatic illness has been a recognized phenomena in the history of people. If we can't get along with our civilization, then we can't get along with ourselves. The body, mind, and spirit will not function correctly when interpersonal relationships break down. It is imperative that we learn people skills in order to remain healthy.

WE WILL BE HAPPIER

Peace of mind can be a very good motivation to develop people skills. Who wants the constant friction that comes from bad relationships that destroy happiness? I knew a woman who loved her husband very much, but she drove him away from her by tactless use of words. She didn't know what she was doing until I tape-recorded her conversation and called it to her attention. Many a beautiful marital relationship has been destroyed not from lack of love but by cruel, thoughtless words. Bad relationships destroy rapport and make life miserable.

Recently a little boy of nine came into our home. He was troubled and quite difficult to handle. One day I asked him the simple question, "What's wrong?" He answered, "My mother doesn't love me. She told me to go live with my father. I was no good, just like him." What would we expect a little boy to do when he is treated so badly by his own mother?

Most of the suffering of this world can be directly traced to the poor use of people skills. One of the sweetest animals in all the world is a pit bulldog, but he can be trained to tear off your arm at the slightest provocation. A pit bull can be loving or dangerous according to his training. We live in a world of pit-bull people who can be so sweet but through poor training are tearing out each other's throats. We become unhappy when we can't get along.

It's easy to hurt people and estrange them from relationships with us. If we are not skillful in dealing with people, we may unknowingly hurt them. To make the wheel of human relationships turn smoothly, we need to skillfully apply the proper grease. If we don't, relationships run dry and break, and happiness grinds to a halt.

I have counseled thousands of troubled married couples. Usually the problems are not severe but involve the simple rules of interpersonal relationships. One couple was typical; let's call them Bill and Mary. Bill was a computer technician whose idea of a vacation was to go to a computer show. Mary was a mother and homemaker whose idea of a vacation was to go to the beach. Mary loved to go out to dinner and a show; Bill never went out unless it involved business or the computer club. Mary hated computers and nagged Bill that it wasn't fair for her to go everywhere alone. Bill became quite angry at her demands. After all, he was a good provider and didn't run around. They screamed and yelled and threatened each other. A child could have told them to compromise and to talk nice, but the suggestion was met with he [or she] started it." It took me a long time to teach them three simple rules of interpersonal relationships:

1. Try to see things from the other person's point of view.

2. Accept the things you cannot change.

3. People change faster when you use nice words.

Bill and Mary are now a happy couple, and their kids who were not making it in school now show the results of happiness.

LIFE WILL BE MORE LIVABLE TO THE PEOPLE AROUND US

We are under an admonition from the Lord to love one another, to love our neighbor as ourselves, and even to love our enemies. What greater way to fulfill this fiat than to learn how to get along with people by developing people skills?

My heart has been hurt and my life impoverished as I have watched people suffer from mishandling. Each year in the United States 150,000 people (maybe many more) commit suicide. A large portion of this plague can be laid at the feet of the thoughtless way people deal with people.

I will never forget Dave. His wife curled her lips in scorn and ridiculed him until he said, "Dr. Diehm, life is no longer worth living. I can't stand what she is saying." So Dave ended his life. The sad truth is that his wife was devastated. She loved the man. She never realized how upsetting her treatment was until it was too late.

Tom was another story: he had planned his suicide to the last detail, and then he prayed to God. God told him to stop talking so cruelly and negatively, and then God sent him someone to love. Now he is a happy, fruitful, productive businessman and member of our church.

When we learn how to deal with people, we make life easier and happier for others—why do it any other way?

GOD WILL SMILE ON OUR RELATIONSHIPS

In our home we have two cats, both neutered, who cannot or will not get along with each other. We must constantly keep them separated (one outside and one in). They fight at the slightest provocation. The last vet bill was $105 for stitches. Both cats are well fed, well loved, and well cared for; but they both are going to lose their happy home if they don't stop this expensive fighting.

God must feel somewhat like I do about my cats when He sees the expensive, deadly fighting that we people engage in. I am sure that God longs for us to develop good people skills and live compatibly in the same world.

When angels announced the birth of Christ, they declared, "Peace on earth, goodwill toward people" (see Luke 2:14). There is no reason to suppose that God wants anything less than peace and goodwill. We will please Him if we supply it.

CHECK YOUR SKILL

Remind yourself that the major problems in life come from the failure to deal correctly with people.

Check out the benefits of treating people right:

- Life will go more smoothly.

- We will earn the respect of others.

- People will befriend us.

- We may make more money.
- We will be healthier.
- We will have fewer enemies.
- We will be happier.
- Life will be more livable to the people around us.
- God will smile on our relationships.

CHAPTER 2

GOOD, BAD, AND UGLY WORDS

Don't flatter yourself that friendship authorizes you to say disagreeable things to your intimates. The nearer you come into a relationship with a person, the more necessary tact and courtesy become.

—OLIVER WENDELL HOLMES

- Do you often get in trouble because of what you say?
- Do you have a reputation of being a critic?
- Do you frequently need to defend yourself?
- Do you take pleasure in putting people down when they deserve it?
- Do you like to pass on tidbits of gossip?
- Are people often shocked at the way you word things?

A few years ago in the San Fernando Valley of the Los Angeles area a small five-year-old boy died from a serious disease—it could be called "bad mouthing." One day he said to his stepfather, "Daddy, I can't ever please you. I never do anything right. I want to die."

The mean-mouthed stepfather replied, "Well, die then!" So, according to his mother, the little boy walked into his bedroom, climbed up into his bed, turned his face to the wall, gave up his spirit, and died. When the case came to the attention of the authorities, the stepfather could not be charged with murder because he had not killed the child with blows. He had killed him with words.

Words can and do kill! More people have been injured and damaged by hurtful words than by all the accidents and malicious assaults combined. An ancient childish doggerel goes, "Sticks and stones may break my bones, but words will never hurt me." It is used as a childhood defense against teasing and criticism, but it is not true and it does not work. Bad words break more spirits than stones ever break bones.

GOOD WORDS

Words are the major source of communication between people. Words, as well as deeds, are the best indicator of what's going on inside the human mind. Proper words help cure the mentally ill, but without the esprit de corps of good words, the physically ill also suffer. Most emotional upsets spring from negative, caustic, cruel, judgmental, critical, and condemning words. Words can destroy or heal, distort or straighten, kill or enliven, disable or build, paralyze or enlighten, destroy or save. Good words are the structure of civilization, and bad words bring the holocaust. Words can and do drive people stark raving mad. On the other hand, words—good words—can forever change the lives of people.

In the nineteenth chapter of Revelation, we find a heavenly image of the Son of God seated on a white horse, a symbol of victory, leading the armies of heaven to battle the hosts of hell. A sword proceeding from the mouth of the One on the white horse symbolizes that heaven fights hell with words, not physical violence. Good news or dynamic words or the gospel is the weapon that Christ and His church uses to engage the devil and his demons.

The Book of John begins, "In the beginning was the Word, and the Word was with God, and the Word was God" (NIV). Now we know that John was talking about Jesus, but why did John call Him "the Word"? Because words are infinitely important and of primary significance in dealing with people.

BAD WORDS

People skills include the proper use of words. Many words are good; they inspire, challenge, and make people your friends. Many words, though, are bad, and they animate hostility, activate bitterness, and energize enemies. Words that are ugly and obscene may make people laugh on certain occasions; but they are usually dirty, with sexual connotations, and their effect is to lower your reputation in the eyes of most people.

I remember one time I went to a banquet and sat across the table from the program chairman. The guest speaker told one dirty joke after another. The program chairman laughed until he was blue in the face and had difficulty sitting in his chair. At the end of the program, the chairman leaned over the table and said to me, "He was funny, but that's the last time that foul-mouthed speaker will ever be on our program."

When James Bernard, missionary to the Indians, came to early America, he had a burning desire to convert the Indians to the Christian faith. He asked several Indian medicine men to teach him the language so he could talk directly to the Indians. They conspired against him and taught him vulgar expressions. Whenever Bernard got up to speak to the Indians, they laughed hysterically at his attempt to get divine truths across with unseemly language. It nullified his message. It was not until he learned the proper words to speak of sacred things that he was able to be used by God to convert thousands of Indians.

Bad words are put-down words. Bad words make people feel unworthy, unwanted. Bad words often emphasize racial slurs or pick on people who are different in body size, mental capacity, or physical ability. Bad words make people feel inferior and take away the joy of living.

UGLY WORDS

Ugly words are obscene words that lower the dignity and civilized way of speaking. Ugly words are swear words, curse words, and blasphemous words. These words fill the air with ugly, contaminated sounds. I have heard men and women poison the air with ugly words that turn everything beautiful and sacred into a cesspool.

Many of these ugly-word users say that emergency circumstances and a certain type of situation demand coarse barnyard words. Colin Powell said in his book *My American Journey* that he used obscenities to deal with and motivate hard, tough men in the service who would only respond to violent language. I think that a person can talk tough without using swear words; but if such words are necessary, it is an exception, not the rule.

Often the use of offensive words is a habit that can be broken when the person is aware that he or she is doing it. When I was in high school, I developed the habit of the extensive use of obscenities. One day a friend said, "Billy, you can't even talk without swearing. It offends me." After three friends and a teacher rebuffed me, I began a program to clean it up. It didn't take long, and the benefits were refreshing.

One time while listening to a daughter talk, I counted her use of the superfluous phrase "you know" twenty times in two minutes. She began an immediate program to change, and she did. Once I also heard a minister repeat this same phrase, but I didn't have the courage to tell him how annoying it was. It isn't always easy to remind a respected person of their misuse of the language. It's even more difficult to confront someone about his or her use of ugly words.

Convicts in prison often have a unique vernacular filled with colorful expressions which they spice up with unnecessary repetitive curse words. As a psychologist conducting group therapy, I never reacted with shock to their shocking language (that would have only encouraged them more). I would often laugh at their unusual idioms and then say, "The swear words distract from the impact of your unique phraseology." Well, I didn't say it like that, but I let them know that swear words are useless, offensive, and defenseless.

The constant use of God's name in vain is particularly repugnant to me. When a person carelessly expresses such language, we must be careful in our corrections, unless we wear the robe of the prophet. Corrections must be delivered softly and nonjudgmentally. If you don't swear, people will soon pick up the idea that you don't like it. Give people a chance to grow and change.

ELIMINATE THE BAD

If you are using bad words that offend people, there are a number of ways to help you make a change:

1. Become aware of your speech and its effect on others. Awareness requires feedback. Before other people take the matter into their hands to correct you, ask them. When you ask for feedback, prepare yourself to listen and strengthen your resolve not to get your feelings hurt, no matter what. If you can't stand criticism, then your only recourse is to tape-record your speaking and listen to yourself.

2. Make a list of the offensive words that you use. Spend some time working on the coarse words one at a time. If the words are racial slurs, perhaps you have a bad attitude toward people you don't understand. During our war with Japan, it was common usage to call the Japanese people "Japs." In the heat of battle, racial slurs are understandable, but when we are trying to get along and make peace, racial slurs have no place. They are a put-down and lead to hostilities.

3. Ask a friend to remind you when your words become bad. We have friends so that we can be ourselves, let down our guard, and relax. A friend constantly nagging and picking on us would be a drag. However, suggestions made infrequently, mutually, and lightly can be a lot of fun.

4. Use fines and rewards to recondition your words. My lifelong friend Dean W. Berger and I played a friendly game of self-improvement. We listed the bad and ugly words we vowed to use no more, and then we fined each other when a violation occurred. Like playing a game of golf, by the end of the day the one with the lowest score won and was treated to some goody like a milkshake. We soon cleaned up our language.

5. Keep reminding yourself of the consequences of hurting people. Bad words and racial slurs can cause permanent damage. Everyone talks about cleaning up crime. Bad words and juvenile delinquency go together—children who turn bad usually have bad mouths. Ugly obscenities may deceive us into thinking that we are big, tough people. The truth: cursing takes away greatness and makes us little, not big; weak, not tough.

6. Deliberately use good words in all occasions. Henry Kissinger, secretary of state and national security advisor during the Nixon administration, tried to stop the war with Vietnam at the Paris peace talks. Dr. Kissinger was a study in careful speech. He uttered each word with utmost care. He knew the value and the weight of words. We don't have to copy him, but we surely need to think before we speak. Deliberately choose and use good words, particularly when the conversation is important.

7. Creatively use milder substitutes for ugly obscenities. Phrases like "oh shoot," "doggone it," "fiddlesticks," or "gee whiz," are better than the harsher ones. When I was trying to cure my use of swear words, I used such phrases as: "You alabaster brown immortal," "oh, unsaturated fatty acid," "ding-dang," and "horny toad." When said with an angry loud tone of voice, the words are quite effective in releasing frustration. People are sometimes shocked with the sounds, but they can't say you are using curse words.

When angry and ugly words start to burst forth, I have said, "Woe is me! for I am undone; because I am a man of unclean lips, and I dwell in the midst of a people of unclean lips." This Scripture quotation (Isa. 6:5) said in a strong boisterous voice often brings a smile rather than a frown. It also releases me. I believe the Lord will forgive me for using sacred language for an earthly cause.

Some people do not have much trouble with swear words, but for those who do, substitutes will help.

ACCENTUATE THE GOOD

Good words have three important characteristics:

1. Good words are kind words. They are delivered without innuendo, sarcasm, or harsh tone of voice. Kind words connotate the gifts of the Spirit: love, joy, peace, patience, kindness, goodness, faithfulness, and self-control. Kind words are not angry words. Anger is in the tone, not in the word itself. You can take a word like *lovely* and speak it with anger or sarcasm and turn the meaning into "ugly." Kindness must come from the heart and be backed by facial expression, body movement, and tone of voice. For example, if one were to say "that's nice" in response to a gift, and say it with a rising inflection and a nasty tone, a person would think it meant "that's not nice." Kind words must be delivered with a kind affect.

2. Good words must be known and understood for them to be useful. One day a nice lady was criticizing herself. She said, "There's nothing good about me." I interrupted and said, "There are lots of good things about you. For example, you are monogamous." Now I was using that word to mean that she was a faithful wife. She burst into tears and cried out, "Why did you call me that?" She did not know the word and thought I was calling her a bad woman.

We may use a perfectly good word, but if it is misinterpreted, that good word can become a very bad one. To tell you the truth, I don't think I ever convinced this lady that *monogamous* was a good word. We may not win them all, but we need to try. Make sure the good words from your mouth are also good to others' ears.

3. Good words must be apropos, in a category in which honesty and sincerity fit nicely. It is not appropriate to tell a person who can't swim that he or she is a good swimmer, anymore than it would be to tell a man without legs that he is a good runner. If your child has just failed a course in math, it would be inappropriate to tell her that she is a good mathematician. You may hug her, tell her that you love her, and point out something she is good at, but you can't tell her something dishonest without harming her perspective of life. If you conjure lies to make people feel good, they will eventually lose faith in you.

Check Your Skill

It is quite satisfying to hear someone practice the niceties of our culture. Saying "please" and "thank you" will never wear out the pleasure of its welcome. My grandparents taught me to be courteous and say "please" and "thank you" when I was just a little boy. I am happy that they did. It's such a little thing, and yet it can be so important. Robert Browning once said, "Oh, the little more, and how much it is! And the little less, and what worlds away!" The difference between being polite and being rude makes a world of difference.

Practice the proper use of words, and you will be well on your way to the mastery of people skills.

CHAPTER 3

SEVEN WORDS THAT CAN REVOLUTIONIZE YOUR PEOPLE SKILLS

We ought to hear at least one little song every day, read a good poem, see a first rate painting, and if possible speak a few sensible words.

—JOHANN WOLFGANG VON GOETHE

Dynamic words breathe, move, and live with such energetic force that they have an impelling potential to change and improve our interpersonal relationships. Here are a few of them:

PHENOMENOLOGY

I am not suggesting that a person should go around saying "phenomenology, phenomenology, phenomenology." I am saying that the word *phenomenology* has a special meaning that when understood and practiced will make a great deal of difference in how we deal with people.

Philosopher Immanuel Kant coined the word we know as *phenomenology* to express the idea that things are not as they are but as you see them. For example, if I see a big black

25

shadow and think it is a big black bear, I am going to respond to the shadow as if it were a bear. The real truth, the "noumenon," or the thing itself, is not as important as how you perceive it. Truth is how a person sees it, not how it is. So, to understand people, and hence to be better able to deal with them, we must realize that everyone reacts to events only as they perceive them.

In an ancient story, four blind men were asked to describe an elephant. The first blind man ran his hand over the elephant's side and said, "An elephant is like a wall." The second blind man grabbed the elephant's leg and said, "An elephant is like a tree." The third blind man seized the elephant's tail and said, "The elephant is like a snake." The fourth blind man touched the elephant's tusk and said, "The elephant is like a sword." On and on we could go, each one of us blind people, describing and relating to an object as we discern it. The elephant's true identity (the "noumenon") is important, of course; but to understand blind men (all of us), we must understand that we react to the "elephant of life" by the part we are allowed to experience. If you don't understand this principle, you can't understand people. The truth is not as important as how the other person sees it, feels it, or understands it.

The great White Light of God, the total truth of how it really is, strikes the earth in blazing glory. No one can ever stare straight into the sun, let alone the White Light of God. So, the great White Light of God filters to the earth as a prism refracts light into the colors of the rainbow. Perhaps I see the White Light of God as being purple in color. That's my phenomenology. Instead of loudly proclaiming, "The White Light of God is purple" (i.e., "An elephant is like a snake"), how much more illuminating it would be to say, "Let me share my purple experiences with you, and you share your orange experiences with me, and together we will know more about the White Light of God." Unfortunately, people are not like that. So we must recognize the inclination of loud, stubborn voices proclaiming that they know exactly what an elephant is all about and that all the White Light of God is refracted into their particular color. That's the way people are. They are inclined to react vigorously to how they see things, how they hear things, and how they feel things. The wise person opens his eyes, becomes aware that other people's feelings and perceptions can be different, and makes allowances for those differences.

ZEITGEIST

Zeitgeist springs from the German language and means "spirit of our times." It is another word that can change our way of getting along with people. Zeitgeist implies that if a person rebels, goes against, or ignores the spirit of our times, he will surely fail. He will fail because he ignores the law of cause and effect—the way things are.

The zeitgeist of an automobile tells us that it takes gasoline to run the machine. Suppose a person says, "Nonsense, gasoline costs a dollar fifty per gallon, while water is less than ten cents a gallon. I'll put water in my gas tank because it's easier to get and, therefore, will be more economical. Besides, in my opinion, the car ought to run on it." The fact, or zeitgeist, is that the car won't run on water. All the "should be's," "ought to be's," and "must be's" in the whole wide world cannot change the zeitgeist—the spirit of how it is.

Dale Carnegie put it like this: "Cooperate with the inevitable." There are many people who spend endless hours griping and complaining about our system—how it isn't fair, and how it ought not to be. "Ought to be's" are a ridiculous waste of time. Many people constantly attack the system because it does not give them what they want. Those who use the word *zeitgeist* figure out the system and cooperate with it. Believe it or not, the system does not play favorites. It gives to people who understand, accept, and work with the way things are. If we cannot cooperate with the way people are, we probably could not cooperate if people were as we think they ought to be.

I know a man who raises German shepherds to be guard dogs. He cooperates with the nature of the German shepherd.

The dogs interpret any sudden motion as a threat. So, the zeitgeist of a friendly relationship with these dogs is smooth, calm movements. The person who uses jerky movements and sudden voice changes ends up with a dog bite.

My point is this: you can't raise camels, children, amoebas, molecules, governments, or German shepherds without taking into account their nature and cooperating with it. Everywhere we go, let our word be *zeitgeist*—"I am cooperating with the nature of people, and, lo and behold, people will cooperate with me."

SERENDIPITY

Horace Wadpole, in his book *The Three Princes of Serendip*, set down the serendipity principle: "You get what you look for." If you look for good, you will get good. It may not be that you will get exactly the good you are looking for; but if you are looking for the good, you will get some variation of good.

Many times people do not see good because of the color of the lenses through which they look. Often they project. A projector is a machine that has a tiny celluloid picture in front of a light. It projects a picture onto a screen outside itself. The true picture is inside. The blown-up picture that everyone sees is out there somewhere. So, if we have difficulty when looking for the good, and all we see is huge pictures of bad, it may be that we have to change the small celluloid slide that lurks within. Literature abounds with illustrations of driven people who search everywhere for holy grails and acres of diamonds only to find them in their own backyards. If we have eyes to see and hearts to believe, we can find lots of good right where we live.

The proper psychological posture consists of the position "I'm OK, you're OK." It means: we see good in us; hence, we see good in others. The serendipitous person looks for good everywhere she goes; therefore, she finds it lodged in herself. It's simple—we get what we look for.

I believe it is important to arrange our lives in terms of priorities and search for those things that will give the greatest satisfaction and the most happiness in the time we have on this earth. It is hard to conceive how anyone can receive benefits from taking vengeance, putting people down, playing games to manipulate, defrauding, cheating, lying, or stealing. When we violate any of the rules of fair play and justice that are written into the structure of the universe, we hurt ourselves and others. Ugly conduct automatically breeds ugly people who give everyone, including themselves, a rough time in life.

There is nothing more satisfying than to search for good qualities and to model behavior that adheres to the highest standards of excellence. Search for the good, and it will come to you, full measure, pressed down and running over. Be serendipitous.

HEURISTIC

From serendipity we go to a cousin word that can also help us deal with people—*heuristic*. It simply means to select the best, to choose the good out of any subject. Everything is made for a purpose. Nothing is totally evil or totally useless. Some people consider an apple, for example, to be good and a snake to be bad. Hence, they are always getting hurt by the bad in the apple, and they are unable to be blessed by the good in a snake.

When we eat the most beautiful Washington red delicious apple, we become aware of the fact that the body knows and uses the word *heuristic*. The body will take the nutrients from the apple and use them to sustain life. The waste matter in the apple will pass out through the digestive system. In other words, the body is heuristic. It selects the good and eliminates the bad.

Truthfully, I am not sure what value can be found in snakes. Perhaps they eat pesky rodents and have their part in the system of ecological balance that keeps our world going. I am not fond of snakes, but I am sure that, with a little thought, good can be found even in an odious reptile. Recently, I read that some doctors were milking poisonous snakes and using the venom for medication to cure a formerly incurable disease. That's what heuristic means—to separate the good from the bad by milking the good out of even a venomous situation.

Why is it that we are so quick to label things and people good or bad? Someone once said: "There is enough bad in the best of us, and enough good in the worst of us that it does not behoove the rest of us to criticize any of us."

All people have some good—let us search for it. That is being heuristic.

TELEOLOGY

Teleology comes from the Greek word *telos* which means "end" or determined by the end. Another similar Greek word, *teleskopos*, means "far seeing" or bringing closer a distant object. Teleology can mean, "Your present is determined by your future" or "if your hope for the future is big, your success for today is great."

Robert Schuller, pastor of the Crystal Cathedal Church in Garden Grove, California, coined the phrase "possibility thinking." We will be more successful in dealing with ourselves and others if we see the possibility of the future. No hope for the future means hopelessness today.

A person's look at his possibilities, his teleology, is as important to his present existence as his biography, his look at the past. Psychologists spend a lot of time in a person's biography, believing that life's experiences make men and women who they are. They teach and preach that good parenting makes good children, and that if we adequately train our children and give them a fine biography, they will turn out to be excellent citizens. I would not deny the truth of the influence of biography. To adequately understand people, we must gather data on their pasts; however, we have often underestimated their possibilities, the value of a person's teleology—his goals, aspirations, and plans for the future.

We cannot live in the past—it is over—and perhaps the future may never come. Still, our present existential moment is largely determined by what we plan to do with our lives—our possibilities.

Our future demands that we set goals. Without goals, the game of life seems boring, unchallenging, and not worthwhile. I have counseled extensively many suicidal people who were struggling to live with no hope for the future.

The Bible talks about three great words that back up profound ideas concerning life. The words are *faith*, *hope*, and *love*. Without faith, there is no meaning; and without love, there is no happiness. *Hope* has been a neglected word, but without hope there is no future. Our teleology is our hope for the future, and without it there is no reason for faith or love. Take away hope, and we die of a common disease known as "give-up-itis."

Many people believe it wrong to make plans for the future. They get this idea from a misinterpretation of a biblical concept, "Take therefore no thought for the morrow, sufficient unto the day is the evil thereof" (Matt. 6:34). Note very carefully what the statement actually says. We are not to plan for any evil tomorrow. Tomorrow is a time for good. That's exactly what teleology says and what hope confirms. We plan for good things to happen to us in the future. That means we have hope. We never count on any bad thing to come our way tomorrow. The evil we take one day at a time, but the good we stretch throughout all eternity.

Set for yourself large teleological goals. Hope with all your might and mind for the realization of your fondest dreams. Set your aspirations on everything good, prosperous, and heavenly. Let tomorrow be a magnificent, overwhelming, lovely, beautiful, stupendous, glorious, compelling, and happy place.

When we see people as possibilities, we are much less judgmental and find it easier to get along with them. We can see the future as a great possibility, and that fills us with hope and optimism—that's teleology.

I believe the most life-changing term of all time for a person's personal happiness and winsome charm in dealing with people is the word *teleology*—large hope for a happy future.

SYNERGETIC

The synergetic principle is both simple and complex. An analogy will best illustrate it. Let us start with a one-cylinder engine that can produce ten horsepower. If eight of these ten-horsepower engines are connected to a single crankshaft, it might be expected that 8 x 10 would produce 80 horsepower. Not so, for the law of synergism increases on a different dimension than multiples. Eight ten-horsepower engines put together to work synergetically will produce 285 horsepower.

One of the generals under Alexander the Great was a Greek named Xenophon. He led an army of 25,000 highly disciplined, cooperative, well-trained soldiers against a Persian rabble of 3 million men. The odds were 120 to 1. Now, I have never heard of any one man who could stand up to 120 in hand-to-hand combat, but according to the chronicles of Xenophon's *Anabasis*, the synergetic Greek soldiers walked through the vastly superior forces of the Persians, killing them by the thousands. The Greeks hardly lost a man. Xenophon defeated the rabble so decisively that the Persian empire collapsed, leaving no doubt whatsoever in anyone's mind who had the superior force. Synergism—cooperative energy—is a powerful force.

A guard at an institution for the criminally insane was once asked a provocative question, "Aren't you afraid? There are only a half-dozen guards against a thousand criminally insane. If these people got together, they could overwhelm you." The guard responded with a smile, "No need for fear; crazy people never cooperate."

No man is an island. No man stands alone. Work together and make things happen. Be synergetic.

ENTROPY

The engineering world brings us another interesting word that has application to human personality. That word is *entropy*. Simply stated, entropy is the amount of energy unavailable for work when the temperature, pressure, and density of the machine rise.

In other words, the more energy the machine takes to run itself, the less energy is available for work. As a behavioral scientist, I can state entropy in terms of human engineering: The more emotional, mental, and physical energy the person uses to run his system, the less energy is available for creative work.

If a Bengal tiger is chewing on your leg, and someone comes up and asks you, "What is two times two?" you probably could not come up with the answer. Even more than that, you wouldn't care. Your whole system would be involved in fighting the tiger, and there would be no energy available for creative work—that's the rule of entropy.

How does this rule apply to people skills? If a person has a serious problem, he or she will not have the strength to deal with anyone or anything. We must help people find personal healing before we expect them to get along. If all our life throbs in the heat and energy of emotional, mental, physical, spiritual, or interpersonal conflict, no strength or energy remains for peace on earth, goodwill toward people.

One of the saddest stories I have ever read concerns the late Howard E. Hughes, a billionaire recluse who, though he could afford to buy three new restaurants a day, died basically of malnutrition. Though he could purchase unlimited pleasure, he wasted away—a shriveled, emaciated, scraggly-bearded, apathetic, unpleasured being. He had everything, yet he had nothing. The law of entropy does not allow us to enjoy anything if we are all fouled up with our own personal set of Bengal tigers.

How do we get rid of our "tigers"? The world is full of suggestions: prayer, therapy, meditation, books, hard work, TLC, medication, exercise, hobbies, friends, and so forth. When stress becomes too difficult to bear, solutions can be found everywhere. Some people solve their own problems. Some people seek professional help. Some people find the answers in the spiritual. What better source than the healing power of

Christ? However, all the solutions have a common factor: you must want help to get help.

Once we escape our "tigers" and have our emotional traumas under control, we will be better able to develop the skills necessary to help, heal, and deal with people. We have composed ourselves, so we can lead others.

IN A NUTSHELL

Remember these words and provocative ideas that will revolutionize your people skills:

- *Phenomenology*—see the other person's point of view. Practice listening to be sure you understand what the other person means.

- *Zeitgeist*—cooperate with the inevitable. Practice holding your tongue when you can't change things. Don't criticize a leopard's spots.

- *Serendipity*—look for the good; you will find it. Practice, at least at first, looking for the good in people.

- *Heuristic*—separate good from bad; find good in bad. Practice finding good, even in hopeless situations.

- *Teleology*—plan for good in the future. Practice being optimistic about what is going to happen tomorrow, and take evil one day at a time.

- *Synergetic*—work together and make things happen. Practice being a cooperative team player whenever you can.

- *Entropy*—deal with your problems to get strength for others. Practice getting yourself together well before you attempt to heal others.

CHECK YOUR SKILL

Search the world over for powerful words backed up by dynamic ideas—words like *faith, hope, love, salvation, integrity,* and *contentment*. Practice thinking, speaking, and living great, authoritative, God-honoring words.

PART II

TEN ESSENTIAL PEOPLE SKILLS

CHAPTER 4

ON BEING CHEERFUL AND HAPPY

A man has made at least a start on discovering the meaning of human life when he plants shade trees under which he knows full well he will never sit.

—ELTON TRUEBLOOD

- Do people often call you a grump?
- How often do people come up to you and say, "Smile"?
- Does your sour disposition make people think you are sick?
- Do you go to church and not participate in worship?
- Do you go to plays and shows and not laugh when others do?
- Do parents or loved ones often say, "What's wrong, Dear?"

It has been said that happiness is a choice, and so is cheerfulness. Viktor E. Frankl in *Man's Search for Meaning* said, "We who lived in the concentration camps can remember the men who walked through the huts comforting others, giving away their last piece of bread. They may have been few in number, but they offer sufficient proof that everything can be taken from a man but one thing: The last of his freedoms to choose one's attitude in any given set of circumstances, *to choose one's own way.*"

CHOOSE CHEERFULNESS AND HAPPINESS

People make the mistake of trying to eliminate all troubles, pains, sorrows, and adversity before they choose to be happy. Cheerfulness and happiness can be obtained before money, power, prestige, success, or fame. In fact, money and fame don't automatically make people happy; happiness has to come from within. We can be pleasant even when loaded with miseries.

Can you think of any person you would rather not be around than a complainer, and can you think of any person you would gravitate more toward than a cheerful, happy person who has a good attitude?

Crotchety, grumpy, mean-spirited people are hard to cope with and don't win many friends. Of course, if they are funny characters like in the movie *Grumpy Old Men,* then we can delight in the humor; but grumpiness directed toward an individual gets unbearable quickly.

Perhaps too much cheerfulness in the midst of adversity can also be painful. We don't want to be guilty of laughing at someone's sorrow.

I suppose it can seem phony if we act cheerful all the time, even when we are not. The Bible tells us that we are to weep with those who weep and rejoice with those who rejoice, so a proper affect is in order. Still, if I had to choose between being a weeping prophet or a cheerful one, cheer seems good to me.

Don't forget that cheerfulness, like happiness, is a choice. In fact, cheerfulness is just one manifestation of happiness. In order to be happy, one must be cheerful. One of the big syndromes in the field of medicine and mental health is clinical depression. It shows itself in sleep apnea, chronic tiredness, and lots of symptomatic aches and pains. Antidepressant drugs as a cheap and easy way to cure depression are all the

rage, but they have side effects and constantly lose their effectiveness. Lots of people have committed suicide while taking
large doses of antidepressants.

We often forget the bottom line: when we constantly
choose to respond to life in a sorrowful, hopeless way we set
within ourselves a pattern of moodal depression that can lead
to clinical depression. It is so easy to constantly look at the
half-empty glass that we never get to enjoy our half-full glass
of water.

REWARDS OF CHOOSING TO BE CHEERFUL

Although choosing to be cheerful most of the time is difficult, it has some significant rewards.

You will have better health. The body of a cheerful person is
healthier and can fight disease better than the body of a
grump. Norman Cousins was hired by UCLA Medical Center
to teach cancer patients how to laugh and be happy as a major
tool in the battle to get the immunization system more active
against cancer. Cheerfulness can add years to your life in the
prevention and healing of disease.

Cheerfulness is a positive influence. Cheerfulness and grumpiness are both contagious. Which would you rather catch? It
goes without saying that most people like to be around the
cheerful person. So the upbeat person will usually have the
most influence and cultivate the most friends.

What would a college football game be like without cheer-
leaders. They are certainly not gloomy. They whip up the
players and the crowd to the highest levels of excitement and
achievement. That's what the cheerful do.

When my sister was in the hospital dying of cancer, the last
words she spoke to me were, "I'm going to make it, Bill." A
wonderful welcome awaits such an optimistic, cheerful Christian in her heavenly home! For the past twenty years I have
cherished my sister's last words. When anything goes against
me, I just remember how pleasant and cheerful she was when
she died.

HOW TO CHOOSE HAPPINESS

How do we acquire this cheerful, optimistic, upbeat attitude that brings a blessing to so many people?

Some people think that in order to be cheerful and happy everything must go our way. One of the most unhappy, cheerless persons I have ever met was a young millionaire who owned the largest yacht in Newport Harbor. He committed suicide. Being rich, healthy, and popular does not bring good cheer. Winning a large lottery has nothing to do with an encouraging attitude. Like anything else of value, we must work hard to develop a pleasant personality. I have never seen anything of value that could not be mastered by diligent effort. Here are some steps to help us choose to create an attitude of happiness and an affect of good cheer.

Find out how you are coming across. I remember teaching music in a small country school where the high school and grade school were in the same building. One day a little fourth-grade girl who came to see me said, "Mr. Diehm, I like you, and it hurts me to hear what the kids are saying about you."

I smiled and responded, "And what are they saying, Dear?"

She was very embarrassed and reluctant. Finally, she said very shyly, "They are making fun of you for the way you yell at the band."

I thought, *Who wouldn't yell at those unmanageable incompetents?* But I said, "Thank you for telling me, Dear." I really was thankful and did try to change. If the kids are making fun of you, it really cuts down your influence in the school.

If you don't get some fairly accurate feedback from those around you, you can't expect to know how you are relating. Ask your friends, listen to what they say, and at least contemplate making some changes.

It pays to come across as a happy, well-adjusted person. If people perceive you as being depressed, sad, withdrawn, cross, or mean, then they will not relate well to you. We must become aware of how we are perceived, but not so aware as to stifle a salty personality. It really only requires a little careful listening and being aware of what is going on around you. Know what people say, but make up your own mind as to what to do about it.

Deliberately practice being what you want to be. If you want to be a happy, cheerful person, then set your mind to act that way. The common theory of emotions is that actions follow feelings, but William James pioneered the theory that feelings follow actions. You don't have to follow your feelings, you can act like you want to feel.

Under most circumstances good cheer is the way to go. Knowing that it is a choice and then being aware of how other people perceive you, set your mind to it and diligently practice the cheerful mode. Sometimes when I have been sharp and snappy with my words, I find it helpful to humble myself and apologize. To say, "I'm sorry, I didn't mean to be that cross," helps me not to do it so readily.

Benjamin Franklin in *The Autocrat of the Breakfast Table* tells of making lists of his virtues and failings and then checking to see how often he succeeded or failed. Maybe that's why he was such a great man—he worked at developing a pleasant personality. Maybe we can't all be Ben, but every little thing we do to improve our disposition will benefit us and the people around us.

Take time to have fun. My brother Bryan attended a Rams and Raiders NFL game. He yelled, screamed, shouted insults, and jumped up and down. His wife thought he made a spectacle of himself. In fact, the woman in front of them turned around and exclaimed, "Cool it, it's only a game." My brother shouted right back, "Not to me, it ain't."

A lot of people are not cheerful because they have difficulty enjoying anything, even a game. I think my brother was enjoying himself, but we must be careful that our fun doesn't become too serious and abrasive to others.

I recommend that people *re-create* themselves through recreation. Have fun, develop a sense of humor, and enjoy yourself—it's later than you think. There are four things we can practice that will help make life fun: (1) smiling, (2) laughing, (3) singing, and (4) playing.

1. A good place to begin is to learn how to *smile*.

> Smile at each other,
> smile at your wife,
> smile at your husband,
> smile at your children,
> smile at each other—
> it doesn't matter who it is,
> and that will help you to grow up
> in greater love for each other.
>
> —Mother Teresa[1]

Often we have taken a baby in our arms who is fussing or crying and tried by cooing, clucking, and tickling to get her to smile. We know intuitively that a smile is better than tears. Whatever it takes, we need to do it and encourage ourselves to smile.

I have experimented on my doctor. When I go into his office with a frown on my face, he instantly says, "I see you don't feel well today; what's wrong?" If I deliberately put a smile on my face, no matter how sick I am, he will say, "I'm glad to see you looking so well." A smile will make a difference in how people perceive you.

2. *Laughter* is usually evidence of a cheerful person, so cultivate it. I collect jokes (clean ones) and tell them to people I think will appreciate them. I laugh heartily at jokes, even if I've heard them before. People who say, "ugh," or "that's terrible," or "I've heard that before," or some other negative comment are practicing a life of bad temper. No sense of humor means no happiness.

Abraham Lincoln was a profoundly serious man with many heavy burdens. His classic statements that surround his statue

---

1. Mother Teresa, *Chicken Soup for the Soul*, Cornfield and Hanson, eds. (Deerfield Beach, Fla.: Health Communications, Inc., 1993), n.p.

at the Lincoln Memorial are awe inspiring. Yet Lincoln had a great sense of humor. The White House rang with the sound of his laughter. He loved to laugh at and tell jokes. We need to laugh—heartily and more often.

3. Like King David we need to *sing* to help ourselves become people after God's own heart. The chorus to the hymn "His Eye Is on the Sparrow" goes, "I sing because I'm happy, I sing because I'm free." This could also be stated as "I'm happy and free because I sing." Singing releases tension, exhilarates the soul, and brings a pleasant atmosphere to the gloomiest of places. That's why the apostle Paul sang when he was thrown into prison.

My best friend did immeasurable harm to me with no intention. He took me aside and said, "Bill, whatever you do, don't sing in public." He knew what I didn't know. I sing off-key and sound like a crow. I had been cheerfully singing at every occasion. I guess I thought people were smiling at me because I was so cheerful. When I was told that I was a crow, I stopped singing. How sad life became; I stopped laughing and smiling too.

One day it all changed when the still small voice of God spoke to me and said, "Bill, crows have as much right to sing as nightingales, and they both will die if they don't sing." I went back to singing and happiness.

4. To *play* is to stay young. Have you ever noticed the young of all the animals of the earth—how they frisk around and play. We assume that they play because they are young. Perhaps we would stay young longer if we continued to play. I know life is hard, and it takes a lot of strength to get ahead and do our work. But occasionally, maybe once a day, we need to let down our hair and frisk around.

The schizophrenics at Lake Washington Mental Hospital were standing around like zombies, as schizophrenics are prone to do. One staff member decided these poor introverts needed to play softball. The staff gathered together and forced the mentally ill through the acts of playing. Soon they dropped the deadly serious schizophrenic stance and began to shout, "Play ball!" Play whether you feel like it or not, and soon you will feel like it.

Remind yourself of the promises in Scripture. The Bible tells us that when we are dealing with ourselves and our problems, we are to:

- "Rejoice in the Lord alway: and again I say, Rejoice" (Phil. 4:4).
- "Finally, my brethren, rejoice in the Lord" (Phil. 3:1).
- "Rejoice evermore" (1 Thess. 5:16).
- "'These things I have spoken to you, that in Me you may have peace. In the world you will have tribulation; but be of good cheer, I have overcome the world'" (John 16:33, NKJV).
- "'Be of good cheer, daughter; your faith has made you well'" (Matt. 9:22, NKJV).
- "Rejoice, O young man, in thy youth; and let thy heart cheer thee in the days of thy youth" (Eccl. 11:9).
- "But none of these things move me, neither count I my life dear unto myself, so that I might finish my course with joy" (Acts 20:24).
- "I have learned, in whatsoever state I am, therewith to be content" (Phil. 4:11).
- "'The LORD gave, and the LORD has taken away; blessed be the name of the LORD'" (Job 1:21, NKJV).
- "Yea, though I walk through the valley of the shadow of death, I will fear no evil: for thou art with me; thy rod and thy staff they comfort me" (Ps. 23:4).

The Bible encourages us to live a life full of joy, good cheer, and happiness. Jesus said, "I am come that they might have life, and that they might have it more abundantly" (John 10:10).

CHECK YOUR SKILL

When we keep close to the Word and our Christian faith, we just can't help but be filled with joy, happiness, and good cheer, and that is a very strong people skill. Isn't it exciting to realize that with practice you can choose to be happy and cheerful? What have you got to lose but unhappiness—and who needs more of that?

Make a list of five ways you could produce happiness within yourself, and do them one by one.

Spread love everywhere you go: first of all
in your own house. Give love to your children,
to your wife or husband, to a next door neighbor.
Let no one ever come to you without leaving better
and happier. Be the living expression of God's
kindness; kindness in your face, kindness in your
eyes, kindness in your smile, kindness in your
warm greeting.

—Mother Teresa as quoted in
Chicken Soup for the Soul[2]

2. Ibid.

CHAPTER 5

MOTIVATING PEOPLE

Be not angry that you cannot make others as you wish them to be, since you cannot make yourself as you wish to be.

—THOMAS À KEMPIS

- Do you find it difficult to inspire and encourage people?
- Do you have a hard time getting your children to do what you want?
- Do your employees seem lazy and unmotivated?
- Do you have a hard time finishing a job?
- Do you often think that nothing ever seems to get done?
- Do you often find yourself bored with nothing to do?

If you can motivate people, then you have one of the greatest of people skills. Put simply: How do you get people to do what you want them to do? Let's suppose that what you want to have happen will strongly benefit the other person. Even then, it is difficult to motivate people. How do we get people to stop taking drugs, to get a job, to go to school, to tell the truth, to keep their promises, or any number of things that will certainly better them? Sometimes, it isn't easy.

I am constantly amazed at the power over the lives of others that come from Charles Manson, David Koresh, Jim Jones, and a host of wicked ones. How do we account for the motivational skill of Hitler, Stalin, Alexander the Great, Napoleon or . . . . The list is endless. I can't account for it, but there are three simple motivational truths that can help us to stir up the people around us: our spouses, our children, the people at work and play, and, perhaps, even ourselves.

We need to teach and model a faith that is dependent upon a relationship with God, not a hope for material gain. That's motivational.

INSPIRE FAITH

If you want to motivate others, you must think, talk, and be the kind of consistent, righteous, Christlike person who advertises the Lord in an honorable way.

How do we go about inspiring belief? I do not want to get people to believe in me (what a shaky foundation). I try to get people to believe in Jesus Christ and to trust in the Son of God. However, if people have no faith in me, they probably will not believe in the Christ I preach. So, we come back full circle. Even if we are pointing them to Jesus, they must have some faith in us as a signpost.

Here are a few tips that help people to have faith:

SPEAK THE TRUTH

People pleasers try hard to get people to like them; but often, the last person we like and trust is the person who tries to be all things to all people. In order for people to trust us, they must believe in what we have to say. How can that be accomplished? By *speaking the truth*, humbly, as we know it. Nothing inspires confidence and motivates people more than the simple truth.

I remember well a deacon at the Baptist church in San Pedro, California, who never used tact or euphemisms. A lot of people did not like him (he hurt their feelings); but you could depend on him to tell the truth, no matter what. Soon, people in the church, including me, went to him for advice because you could depend on it being straight. He was honest.

Where do euphemisms and tact come in? Of course we can soften the truth. If truth hurts too much, it probably isn't the truth. I like the sandwich approach. The meat of truth is enveloped between two pieces of buttered bread. The raw meat of critical truth is distasteful. So, cook it by thinking it over and carefully phrasing it, and then dish it up with some compliments (buttered bread).

In any case, the raw meat of uncooked truth is more palatable than the slimy taste of rotten lies, so tell the truth and people will believe in you, which will motivate them.

KEEP YOUR WORD

Not long ago, I attended a funeral. A friend of mine, who was very sick, showed up. I exclaimed, "George, you have been very ill, just out of the hospital; why are you here?" He replied, "I promised the deceased man's wife that I would come, and I will keep my promise, even if it kills me." I think he carried it a little too far, but think of all the people who carelessly make promises that they don't bother to keep.

It is particularly damaging to promise your children that you are going to do something and then frivolously break the promise. One time a friend of mine promised his son that he would buy him a Honda motorbike when he graduated from high school. The time came, and the father bought him another brand and saved a few dollars. It seemed such a little thing, but the father and son were estranged from each other, and a relationship was broken.

BE CONSISTENT

One of the ugly words of the world is *hypocrisy*, which is the opposite of consistency. The Bible says, "A double-minded [inconsistent] man is unstable in all his ways" (James 1:8). No one knows for sure which side of his personality he will show today. Faith cannot build in such an atmosphere.

One time I taught in a country school and was very impressed by a particular teacher. I soon found out that the kids hated her. I asked why, and they said, "She's two-faced, sweet to you and sour to us." That type of inconsistency just doesn't work. Science is built on reliability and replication—so are human relationships.

Not long ago a visitor came to church and mouthed a lot of spirituality. I was impressed. My wife and I left church at the same time as our visitor. As we passed his car, he opened the door and began to beat his dog, shouting at the top of his lungs, "I told you not to jump into the front seat." My wife remarked, "He may be a great Christian to our church people, but the dog doesn't think he is one."

BE FAIR AND JUST

Our Constitution calls for a level playing field in the game of life in which everyone has an equal opportunity. When we are unfair we unravel the ball, and the game is not worth playing or watching.

Have you ever taken your car to a garage that overcharged you or did work that did not need to be done? Do you go back to that garage? No! In fact, that garage won't stay in business long if it doesn't change its ways. We expect doctors, lawyers, mechanics, and other people we deal with to be fair and just. If not, we lose faith and trust, and they cannot inspire us or motivate us.

ENCOURAGE OTHERS

Arnold Schwarzenegger, the movie star and bodybuilder, was appointed by President Bill Clinton to head up a national fitness program. When Schwarzenegger visited a physical therapy program for those with spinal cord injuries, a man said, "I can't." Schwarzenegger's reply, "At least you can try," motivated the injured man, and when I read the story, it motivated me. We need to encourage more people (and more often) to try.

When someone says, "I can't do it," you tell them, "Try." There are exceptions to these rules, so we must be wise. It would be cruel to tell a man without legs to run, but it would be equally cruel not to tell a man with artificial limbs to try to walk.

All of his life Marty McArthur had wanted to sky dive. He was thirty years old and had never tried to do it. He was a paraplegic from a spinal injury so everyone told him it was impossible. When a young man who was a paraplegic climbed El Capitan in Yosemite National Park, Marty was inspired. He finally persuaded the pilot of a drop plane to take him to 20,000 feet. Two friends helped him get on his gear and tossed him out of the plane. He had no use of his legs, and so they were broken as they whipped up around his head in the slip stream. One arm was partially useful, but he had difficulty pulling the rip cord. When he finally released the parachute he was so close to the ground that he broke both arms and his shoulder when he landed.

When I visited Marty in the hospital I asked, "Aren't you sorry you did such a foolish thing? You could have been killed." He replied, "No, I'm not sorry. It was a great experience. I know now that I can't do it, but I sure did try." Marty's course is too extreme, and I can't recommend it; but we've got to admit, he sure did try.

ENCOURAGE IN A POSITIVE WAY

If we are going to encourage people, not only must we inspire them to try, but we must *do* it in a positive way. Nothing discourages accomplishment more than negativity. Negative thinking makes people paranoid and focused on the activity of the devil. Constantly tearing down and pointing out insurmountable difficulties makes the evil side seem greater than the good.

The July 1995 issue of *Paraplegia News* featured Stefan Florescu, a sixty-eight-year-old man who has been paraplegic for forty-three years. The former school teacher and lifeguard broke his neck in a diving accident. Since that time he has won many gold and silver medals as a wheelchair athlete, having competed in thirty-five consecutive national wheelchair sports competitions. He helped establish the National Association for Handicapped People and fully participates in community life. He calls the swimming accident in which he cracked the sixth vertebra in his spine "a lucky break." He motivates and encourages people with his positive attitude.

Build on What Is Right

If we are to encourage people and hence motivate them, the last thing in the world that will work is criticism and constantly harping on what is wrong. We motivate people, including ourselves, by building on what is right, not what is wrong.

A long time ago psychology discovered what is called *behavior modification*—rewarding people or animals for proper behavior will reinforce that behavior. Positive reinforcement works much better than negative reinforcement (i.e., punishment or criticism for bad conduct).

In spite of the overwhelming scientific evidence that behavior is modified by rewarding right conduct, we continue to increase our methods of punishment to try to extinguish bad behavior. People work for rewards rather than the avoidance of pain, so we can build successfully on what is right rather than what is wrong.

I remember one time a woman called and whined, "Everything has gone wrong."

I responded, "You don't mean everything; obviously you can still breathe and talk."

"You know what I mean," she cried.

"Yes, I know what you mean, but you don't know what I mean. You are turning something wrong into *everything*, and no one can solve the problems of life if everything is wrong." Then I told her what had been my mother's favorite saying, "Count your blessings, not your curses." That's what it means to build on the right—emphasize it, count it, and put it in first place.

Have you ever noticed how it takes just one sourpuss to ruin a party? Bad temper is so discouraging and so contagious that "Maintain a good disposition" should be written on every marriage license and every birth certificate.

People often use any excuse to be cross and cranky: a headache, sickness, bad events, PMS, losing money, hard work, or any kind of weather. The real test of whether or not a person has a good disposition is not how they act when they win the lottery, but how they react when they declare bankruptcy. It's not the joyous winner but the good loser who proves the quality of his disposition.

July 1995 *Paraplegia News* tells the story of Steve Baldwin who became quadriplegic in 1990 at age forty-four. A jack-knifed trailer slammed into his Harley Davidson while he was riding to a motorcycle rally. He learned that in order to survive he had to find an interest in life and focus on the positive. "I know I'll never walk again or be able to use my hands," he says, "but . . . I can use my mind, voice, and faith to help others."

Steve Baldwin and his wife, Linda, visit patients with disabilities at the VA hospital and the Texas Institute of Rehabilitation and Research in Houston, Texas. They try to help people put their lives back on track. Baldwin says he gets more out of the visits than those in the hospital do. Because of the Baldwins' help, a quadriplegic woman and her husband took their first outing since her accident. Not surprisingly, the Baldwins took the couple to Biker's Weekend at their church.

No matter who you are or what you face, you can be a happy, useful person who maintains a good disposition.

TAKE THE HIGH ROAD OF LOVE

Hate is very motivational, and although it has some quick impact, it will eventually lose out to love. Vengeance can send men screaming into a battle to the death, but forgiveness holds the key to eternal life. Greed can send vast hordes pillaging, looting, and destroying, while generosity builds pleasant towns and loving families. Raw lust can create insane brutality and destroy the souls of men, women, and children, while a monogamous mating instinct in the bonds of marriage is the secret of happiness and perpetuating the species.

It takes just thirty seconds for a modern chainsaw to cut down a magnificent six-hundred-year-old redwood tree. Low-road motivators take the quick and easy route and turn the forest land into a barren desert. High-road motivators plant trees and cultivate them to replace those they cut down.

Whenever you see someone motivating themselves or someone else with low-road methods, you can know that the end will be quick destruction. Some of the low-road methods include hate, guilt, hostility, resentment, vengeance, fear, worry, anxiety, lust, undisciplined sex, jealousy, pride, gossip, self-centeredness, bad memories, over sensitivity, critical attitude, greed, slander, pessimism, negativism, lack of life plan, and lack of contentment. I made a list of more than one hundred low-road methods to motivation, but we need not dwell on the negative. Instead, let's turn to high-road methods of motivation.

THE POWER OF LOVE

The greatest of all high-road methods of motivation is love. *Love* is a many faceted word. In English we use the word *love* to mean anything from liking chocolate, to having sex, to caring for each other and our children, to the profound love which God has for us in Christ. According to *Young's Analytical Concordance to the Bible*, the Bible has thirty-four Greek and Hebrew words that we translate into the one word *love*. When we are not engaged in an in-depth study, we commonly list three Greek words that mean love: (1) *Eros*—pleasurable, desirable, sexual love; (2) *Phileo*—brotherly love and friendship; (3) *Agape*—high-level love of God for people, people for God, and people for each other; altruistic, Christian love.

Love is mentioned in the Bible hundreds of times, and the idea of love is the central thrust of the whole Book. There is no more sacred or profound word. Jesus made agape love for

God the first commandment, and He interpreted God's love for us by His death on the cross.

In the thirteenth chapter of John we read the story of Jesus washing the disciples' feet, a lowly task necessary from the condition of the hot, dusty roads—the task of a meager servant. It was in this chapter that Jesus said, "A new commandment I give to you, that you love one another; as I have loved you, that you also love one another" (John 13:34, NKJV). So, how do we love one another? By doing for each other those meager, lowly tasks that need to be done. Jesus said we ought to wash one another's feet. It is more than a ceremony; it is a principle of love.

The Bible urges us: "Beloved, let us love one another, for love is of God; and everyone who loves is born of God and knows God. He who does not love does not know God, for God is Love" (1 John 4:7–8, NKJV).

I believe that the most effective change in anyone comes through unconditional love. We do not change for our enemies who hate us for who we are; we change for our friends who love us as we are but want to help us continually change and grow into better and more loving people.

GLIMMERS OF HOPE

Low-road methods of motivation lead to hopelessness, but the high road is filled with the supreme optimism of hope. In youth groups I used to sing a song of high hopes entitled "Something Good Is Going to Happen to Me." If we can instill the hope in people of something good coming, they will be able to endure even the most horrendous problems. Dr. Viktor E. Frankl, author of *Man's Search for Meaning*, said he survived the Holocaust death camps by thinking and hoping for the time that he would lecture and write a book about his experiences.

Pope John Paul II wrote a book entitled *Crossing the Threshold of Hope* in which he extols the driving motivation of hope to change the world. Without hope we have despair, but with hope we have courage to face and overcome all obstacles.

If we wish to motivate people, we must find some way to instill hope, a hope that leads to faith that leads to love that leads to God and eternity.

FAITH THAT ALWAYS STANDS

Dr. Douglas Courpron was a missionary to China for over forty years. He told about the rice Christians. As long as you gave them a bowl of rice every day, they were dedicated Christians. That is similar to the prosperity doctrine that says if you are a true Christian, God will materially bless you. I believe that God will prosper His children, but motivational faith must be based on something higher than physical rewards.

Dr. E. Stanley Jones wrote a book entitled *The Divine Yes*. He wrote this book to declare that he loved God and he knew that God loved him, even though everything had been taken away from him. He had suffered a stroke that left him paralyzed, without movement and without speech. Through a system of sign language he communicated, "Anyone can have faith when things are going right; the real test is can you have faith when you are put to the final test, and everything has gone wrong?"

FOLLOW HIS LEADING

When E. Stanley Jones was preparing to commit himself as a missionary to India, his mother confronted him, "Son, if you leave me and go to India, I will die." Jones went into a time of prayer and communication with God and then responded to his mother, "Mother, I love you and I don't want you to die, but God has called me to India and I must go." Jones went to India, but his mother didn't die. Rather, she lived to see her son distinguish himself with fifty years of converting the upper-class Hindus to the Christian faith.

Listening to the voice of God can be dangerous, but *not listening* is terminal. To determine whether or not you are hearing the voice of God, remember that in the first chapter of John, Jesus is called "the Word" or the interpreter of God's message. When you think you hear the message of God, ask yourself, Is this a Christlike voice? Would the life and teaching of Jesus confirm the truth of what I am hearing? Then check out the message with the corporate body of Christ, the church. Ask the pastor and pray with both him and some other devout Christians. When you have checked the message of God with prayer, the teaching of Jesus, and the church, you can be more certain that Satan is not trying to deceive you.

CHECK YOUR SKILL

Sometimes bad people use evil motivational forces that are hypnotic and cause enslaved people to do terrible things; but we are talking about legitimate, open and above-board, honest methods of motivation. To motivate people we must:

- Inspire faith.

  1. Speak the truth.
  2. Keep our word.
  3. Be consistent.
  4. Be fair.

- Encourage others.

  1. Teach "try" instead of "can't."
  2. Avoid negativity.
  3. Build on what's right, not what's wrong.
  4. Maintain a good disposition.

- Take the high road.

  1. The greatest of all is love.
  2. Hope completes faith and love.
  3. A faith does not depend on prosperity.
  4. Let God lead your life.

CHAPTER 6

THE POWER OF CONTROLLED ANGER

All that is essential for the triumph of evil is that good men do nothing.

—EDMUND BURKE

- Do people say you have a temper?
- Are your wife and children afraid of you?
- Does your dog cower and your cat hide when you yell?
- Do little frustrations make you rage and swear?
- Do people avoid you when you get aggressive?
- What do you think? Is your anger under control?

The Bible tells us that "the wrath of man worketh not the righteousness of God" (James 1:20). Yet, it also tells us many times that God became angry at humankind. It seems to me that when anger controls us, we are out of control and become evil. Controlled anger is another thing, though. For example, when Jesus cleansed the temple, His actions suggest a considerable amount of anger. The Bible tells us that He took the time to braid a whip to drive out the animals. Braiding a whip means He delayed action, which most people do when they control anger. So, controlled anger can become a righteous anger, a motivating anger.

We often hear today that we are never to confront our children in anger or, particularly, use physical force in anger. To shut the anger out of our relationships is to shut out one of the most effective emotional forces in dealing with people. If we extinguish our anger, we close down caring; but if anger burns out of command, it turns into a destructive force. Expressing controlled anger will impact our relationships in a powerful way and can be quite effective in dealing with recalcitrant people.

When my father went into a rage, our whole family stood at reverential attention. I suppose that's why he let his temper get the best of him—so he could get the best of us.

Adolf Hitler had raging temper tantrums. Often his generals delayed telling him important information in order to avoid the tantrums. It would have been much more costly for the Allies in the invasion if Hitler had been informed a day sooner. Good for us, but bad for him. If people are afraid of you and your temper, you will pay with a loss of trust.

In the movie *M.A.S.H.* two amateur football teams were playing. A professional was badly upsetting the doctors' side. A doctor said, "I'll take him out." So he taunted the professional until the professional chased him off the field and got kicked out of the game. Uncontrolled anger will get you sidelined in the game of life. Many vicious crimes are committed as a result of uncontrolled anger. Don't correct your kids or have an interchange with anyone when your anger is out of control.

If your anger is thoroughly checkreined and you are firmly in the saddle, then be sure you can win some races and conquer some kingdoms with its power. People do not always like or follow or obey Mr. Goodguy who never uses the emotional thrust of anger to bring control to the management of unruly situations.

HANDLING OUT-OF-CONTROL ANGER

One day I was in a violent temper rage. I can't remember what it was all about, but my son Philip was the recipient of my rage. As I piled accusations and blame upon him he responded calmly but firmly, "What you are saying, Dad, is just not true." I don't think he stopped my rage at the time because when you let your temper go beyond a certain point it breaks a hole in the dike. He did teach me a lesson, though. My memory is filled with the idea that temper and the truth do not go together. When you let your anger go berserk, you can forget about reason, and also truth evaporates like a snowball on a hot summer day.

We've all had the occasion to be confronted by someone whose anger is out of control. Whether at work, at home, or somewhere else, dealing with an angry person tests the strength of our people skills. How do you handle a person whose anger is out of control?

NEVER MEET ANGER WITH ANGER

Most people use the method of trying to out-anger the angry one. Of course, they quickly incur the risk of violent physical confrontation. On occasions a superior force can calm angry outbursts. For example, one time my father was very angry. He was cursing and swearing and driving the car erratically. Suddenly, flashing red lights appeared in back of us, and a policeman pulled us over. My father became instantly calm. Such an overpowering authority can calm an angry person—but it's risky for the rest of us to try.

The best procedure when faced with powerful anger is to speak the calm, noninflammatory truth. Women have often asked me how they can handle their husbands who manipulate them with anger. I have always cautioned them to rarely if ever meet anger with anger. Physical violence is often the result. It is wise to meet passionate anger with loving compliance, but if the angry spouse is wrong, then wait until the anger passes before you confront. For example: the husband screams and rages about the price of a new dress. The reply could be, "I'm sorry you don't like the dress; I didn't realize I was spending so much money. I'll take it back." When he calms down, softly say to him, "Honey, I want to talk to you about the household budget."

If every time you bring up the confrontation you are met with anger, then you know your husband is trying to get his own way the same way a child does—by a screaming temper tantrum. The marriage needs some help.

CHOOSE HOW AND WHEN TO RESPOND

If you're confornted by a person whose anger is out of control, choosing how and when to respond is the first step toward success. Avoid confrontation, if possible, when:

- the other person is having a temper tantrum.
- the other party is drunk, confused by drugs, or mentally ill.
- the other person is preoccupied, stressed out, or dealing with larger priorities.

To unnecessarily confront issues when they are most certainly doomed to failure is not wise. Anything that could be accomplished will surely be undone when normalcy prevails.

If a person has a gun at your head and is making an unreasonable angry demand like "Give me your money!", isn't it rational to suggest that you acquiesce, give your money, and save your life?

I have counseled with people who think that under no circumstances should they surrender. How foolish. When a person is in a violent temper rage, we are not in a position to win the argument. When the time comes and we are in court with the person who took our money, then we are in a position to win the argument.

As a psychologist and therapist, I had many outstanding victories and successes, but I will never forget one of my most dismal failures. A husband and wife loved each other very much, and they had two beautiful children, a boy and a girl. Whenever the wife spoke sweet and nice, her husband gave her anything she wanted, but for some reason the habit of her life was to get her own way through anger. Eventually, she lost. He left, permanently. The children, left without proper guidance, made one bad decision after another and destroyed their lives.

UNDERSTAND THE POWER OF PASSIONS

The passions of anger, fear, sex, and appetite have always been elevated in strong leaders and dynamic men and women. The passions are highly motivational. They can inspire you to climb to the mountaintop or bury you in the deepest pit.

Controlled and directed sex within the bonds of marriage leads to a loving, caring family and home. Sex on a rampage leads to plagues of disease and the devastating destruction of relationships, even civilizations.

Controlled and directed fear leads to a protective environment in which society provides housing, police, medicine, and science to create a comfortable, safe lifestyle. Uncontrolled fear creates madness and paranoid delusions that make people act like lemmings running over a cliff to drown in the sea.

Controlled and directed appetite builds strong, healthy, disciplined bodies, like the temple of God, free from disease. Uncontrolled appetite stifles the body, takes away mobility, brings an apathetic state of mind, and leads to early death.

Controlled and directed anger motivates and drives men and women to cleanse the temple, reform society, and grow the kingdom of God on earth. Uncontrolled anger is a wrecking machine of vengeance and hate that destroys everything in its path.

How important it is to control the passions.

VALUING CONTROLLED ANGER

I don't think there is any place in human relationships for uncontrolled, violent anger. Seldom does any method work against it and never does violent anger build happy relationships. Now controlled anger is another dimension. To raise our voices, to speak firmly and sharply, to let people know we care enough to be angry, to use the force of anger without any abuse can be very good.

We were having a family gathering, and my sister-in-law was under the Christmas tree on her hands and knees arranging the packages. Her husband came up in back of her and whacked her hard on the behind. He laughed as he did it, but obviously it hurt. My sister-in-law rose to her feet and confronted him with a firm, controlled angry voice. "You stop that," she said, "I will not tolerate you hitting me even in fun." He was subdued and apologetic. If she had let it go, who knows. If she had responded sweetly and lightly, I think it would have encouraged his bad behavior. Sometimes we must raise our voice and say, "You stop that. I won't tolerate it." There is no need to feel guilty about controlled anger.

WAYS TO CONTROL ANGER

It is easy to say, "Control your anger, and it will help you deal effectively with people." But the real question is, "How do you do it?"

Treat underlying physical causes. Many physical problems contribute to the lack of controlled anger. For example, a disease like diabetes with attendant hyperglycemia (high blood sugar) can be responsible for temper rages. With medical help like blood tests, insulin, or oral medication, the ups and downs of temperament that come from the fluctuations of blood sugar can be controlled.

There are a number of other physical conditions that can account for anger. Alcohol, even light social drinking, can lower inhibitions and raise combativeness to an abusive level in some people. A popular saying concerning alcohol is, "Don't drink and drive." For people skills, an equally important rule is, "Don't drive if the powerful forces of passionate anger take over." A lot more people than we will ever realize have died that way.

Of course, various types of drugs can cause unpredictable behavior. Many bottles of prescription pills contain a warning against operating machinery while taking the medication. We need to heed the warning. Then we have the problem of illegal drugs, which have killed legions of people by destroying their control systems and letting their emotions rage.

Sickness, pain, and physical trauma are often met by emotional responses such as anxiety, depression, and hostility (which is another way of saying fear, negativity, and anger). My sister had temper rages every month—this was before they had named it PMS. I never excused her for it, but as I look back, I realize that her monthly cycle was a factor in her disturbed moods.

Reduce stress. Physical dysfunction is probably not a total excuse for anger rages, but it cannot be discounted. We must prepare for those times when body weakness contributes to lack of emotional control by reducing stress during those times.

Some people handle excessive stress through fear, anxiety, or worry, some through depression, and others through anger. Excessive stress is a disease-producing, life-threatening, mind-boggling condition. Those who respond to stress with anger are in a lot of danger. If you find yourself blowing up to reduce the pain of stress, quickly find a method further away from the cliff of termination.

Stress-induced uncontrolled anger can be compared to a loaded gun with a hair trigger. If it fires without a proper target, it can do unintended damage. Those who have this hair trigger must take precautions on the path of life. Find out what jars your trigger and prepare to avoid those occasions. Prayer and Christian therapy can provide the safety lock for your trigger and sometimes can even unload the gun.

Practice redirecting anger. Over the years of struggling to control my temper, I have developed a system that works well for me. Whenever I have shared it, it has worked well for others too. I call the system "generation." Spontaneous anger is very difficult to control, so I simply generate a feeling of anger and then control it, usually by getting some important work done. The method is similar to that used by some athletes when their bodies fire adrenaline just before lifting a heavy weight or delivering a karate chop.

I "generate" the feeling of anger by uttering a guttural sound and pounding my fist into the palm of my hand. Like an actor preparing for a part in a movie, I will pound a pillow with a rolled-up newspaper, clench my jaws, and exclaim, "I am angry!" When the feeling of anger floods my system, I then practice methods of controlling it. I generate anger and use it as a motivator to work hard at my computer.

When you arbitrarily "generate" anger, it is much easier to dissipate, direct, and control. Sometimes we deal with important events like a speaking engagement with fear, worry, and nervousness. I have discovered it is more beneficial to greet important occasions with controlled anger. It gives the affect of power and confidence.

Some people greet the idea of "generation" and then dissipation or control of anger with disdain. I admit that the idea isn't for everyone. Those who are in proper control of themselves don't need it. However, for those who do, practicing getting control of your anger will pay dividends later when you need to be in control.

CHECK YOUR SKILL

Uncontrolled anger is a devastatingly destructive force to human relations. *No anger* is equivalent to no care, no love, no responsiveness. Controlled anger is a powerful motivating force and a delightful addition to dealing effectively with one another.

This week practice one of the three ways to control anger. Set a goal. If stress is increasing your anger, set a goal of reducing stress by doing such things as taking a ten-minute walk after supper, spending fifteen minutes reading an uplifting book, or doing some other activity you enjoy.

CHAPTER 7

GIVING AND RECEIVING FEEDBACK

*Have you learned lessons only of those who
admired you, and were tender with you?
Have you not learned great lessons from those
who reject you, and brace themselves
against you?*

—WALT WHITMAN

- Do your children say that you nag too much?
- Do you criticize anything lower than an *A* on a report card?
- When a friend buys a new product, do you point out the bad features?
- Do you listen or defend when others criticize you?
- Are you easily offended and constantly getting hurt?
- Is it said of you, "You can dish it out, but you can't take it?"

A first-grade teacher experimented with the idea that her children would live up to expectations and live down to criticism. She divided the children in her class into those who had brown eyes and those who had blue eyes. She told the class that brown-eyed children were genetically inferior. Soon the brown-eyed children began to misbehave, get poorer grades, and develop symptoms of inferiority.

Then the teacher announced to the class that a mistake had been made. The truth was that brown-eyed children were actually more intelligent than blue-eyed children. Immediately there was a reversal in behavior, grades, and status, which reveals that criticism hurts people more than most of us imagine.

Criticism has caused more unhappiness, shattered more marriages, destroyed more children, discouraged more people, and stopped more progress than any other weapon. Indeed it is an implement of war. When the children of Israel were going through the wilderness on the way to the promised land, their faultfinding, complaints, critical attitude, and lack of faith grieved God and caused them to wander in the wilderness for forty years (see Exod. 32:9–10).

Satan is called the "accuser of our brothers" in Revelation 12:10 because accusation and criticism are his chief weapons. We sadly look at the trend in our media of making people guilty, not by trial, but by accusation. When the sons of God presented themselves before the heavenly throne in Job 1:6, the devil was there to criticize the people on earth. He has a passion for criticism, as do his followers, and we all need to be cautioned.

In an experiment at UCLA Medical Center, problem children were observed as they worked puzzles with their mothers. Whenever a problem child made a mistake, his or her mother would respond with words such as, "You're stupid! You don't know anything!" When a normal or well-adjusted child made a mistake or said, "I don't know," the mother would say, "See, it's a sled," (or whatever it was), and she would continue, "It goes on snow like this. Remember when we went sledding last year?" Mothers of well-adjusted children explained; mothers of problem children criticized. Think of the tremendous amount of problem children we have, and let the thought make you shun criticism.

The word *criticism* means censure, condemnation, reproof, faultfinding, backbiting, blame, disapproval, and judgment— finding fault in a judgmental way. It has very little value in relationships between people.

HOW TO SOFTEN THE
BLOW OF CRITICISM RECEIVED

Criticism differs from confrontation in that it seldom faces the one being criticized. When it does it usually is not looking for a solution but rather lodges a complaint or levels an attack. Rare is the person who can cope with criticism, and rare is the person who gives criticism with a loving heart. Good confrontation is a necessity in developing people skills; criticism seldom is good and often leads to pain, sorrow, and broken relationships.

Unfortunately we often find ourselves on the receiving end of criticism. Then we see firsthand how it can hurt. Also, like war, crime, disease, and misfortune, criticism will always be with us. So we have to learn to see criticism for what it is— and learn that it isn't always bad.

Ask yourself, "Why is this person criticizing me?" We must consider that sometimes the person is trying to express love and commitment. Good parents want to improve and direct the behavior of their children, but if the only time children get attention from their parents is when they do something wrong, they learn that misbehaving is the best way for them to obtain attention.

Don't become too concerned when people mildly correct you. Correcting the failings in others seems to be built into the human race. We have a deep desire to improve ourselves and to correct the wrongs that we see around us. We groom each other and brush the lint off each other's collars. We tell people how to drive and where to park. The problem is a matter of degree. When people try to improve us too harshly or too often, it can become quite annoying and even harmful.

Don't overreact to criticism from leaders. Some people, such as leaders, see themselves responsible for our behavior. Good leaders know how they can get people to do what they want them to do without using harping, carping criticism. People who are not good leaders rudely and crudely point out the mistakes and inconsistencies in others, sometimes to distract attention from their own errors.

Leaders who see themselves as bosses, whose only method of correction is to call attention to the things they do not like, will have poor results in working with people. Those bosses who inspire and encourage will soon surpass them.

Remember that criticism can grow out of an honest desire to improve people. When we reinforce a sincere desire with bitterness, sarcasm, or hateful impatience, the criticism converts from helpful to harmful. If we can hear deeper than the sound of a caustic tongue, we may be able to get the bit of truth out of an attack by a friend or enemy. Harsh criticism is difficult for anyone to endure, but criticism properly administered and received can on rare occasions change our lives for the better.

Recognize that some criticism comes from people with low self-esteem. Putting someone else down by means of criticism is a way by which people try to bolster their own feelings of self-worth. It's like the game of King of the Hill that we played as children—pushing and shoving others until we are on top. Some people think they can get ahead by knocking others down. Don't be too disturbed, because everyone gets pushed down on occasions.

See some criticism as a cry for help. That other person is really not angry at us, but she is ventilating helpless feelings and expressing her own pain. Suffering people often defend themselves by projecting blame. If you keep your cool, the criticizing person may end up in your arms, crying and sobbing.

Avoid responding too vigorously to criticism by stopping and taking a deep breath. There may be an iota of truth in what they are saying. Look for it. Screen out the pain and look for gain. Sometimes surgery is the only way we can be healed. Think of unjust criticism as an attempt to exorcise our faults. Search for that small bit of truth that may be beneficial to you. If somebody's criticism is hitting too close to home—they may be right!

GIVE POSITIVE FEEDBACK, NOT NEGATIVE CRITICISM

Criticism is a very poor vehicle to induce change, to correct, or to help people be better. However, there are ways we can positively influence others to change.

Tell people how you feel, not what they did wrong. Shift the emphasis from the other person to yourself. Instead of saying, "You have a dirty mind and a foul mouth," be a little creative and say, "I get very upset when I am accosted by swear words, and to me dirty jokes attack the sacredness of sex. I would prefer not to hear that stuff." Perhaps the other person has uncharacteristically gone too far. Then say, "I like cute, clever jokes, but that one went too far." The point is, don't attack the person; attack the problem from your viewpoint.

Learn to deliver feedback as a mild, indirect suggestion. The other person will think that the idea was his or hers and quickly change. A harsh question like, "Why haven't you chopped the wood, you lazy bum?" can meet with an assaultive response from some people. An indirect statement, "We need to get the wood in for the winter," is less inflammatory and may be all that's needed to get wood chips flying. It all depends on the person; some people can take a harsh statement and some can't, so be careful.

Never criticize failings without recognizing virtues. When a person does something wrong, he or she often gets punished by guilt, negative feedback, or the legal system. When a person does something right, he or she is often ignored. In a perverse way, such a procedure encourages wrong behavior, because that is what gets attention. Everyone needs to improve, and when the slightest improvement is made, the praise needs to be lavish. At least we need to recognize when a person does the right thing. Then more people will do the right thing.

It is customary to shout at people when they do wrong and whisper or ignore it when they do right. Turn it around. Shout at the right and whisper at the wrong.

Don't gunneysack criticism. That is, don't accumulate a lot of refuse in a garbage bag and dump it on someone's head. If you shoot your whole arsenal at a person, you are likely to blow them away. Deal with sins one at a time; don't collect them. It's simple: If you can't forgive a person for past sins, your own forgiveness will be in doubt. "'For if you forgive men when they sin against you, your heavenly Father will also forgive you. But if you do not forgive men their sins, your Father will not forgive your sins'" (Matt. 6:14–15, NIV). Don't accumulate and go to the past to inundate people with blame—unless you want to make enemies and severely hurt them.

ALTERNATIVES TO CRITICISM

Dialog, confrontation, and feedback are the methods of choice, but we will discuss these techniques in another chapter. Here are some other methods to use before we try the critical approach.

1. Show rather than tell. By watching you, people will gradually see what you are doing and start modeling your behavior. Harsh criticism may stay with them for a lifetime, and they still won't change. Be patient, and by your lifestyle show them what is right.

I had some friends who allowed their cat to roam on the table and lick their plates while they were eating—odious behavior to me. I wanted to remind them that they are not animals, so they shouldn't eat with them. I could have used some hard words about the possibility of the cat carrying some lethal disease. Instead, when the cat approached my plate, I picked up my dinner and walked over to the counter to eat. The people put the cat outside and apologized. I had not said a word.

When people ask you if they can smoke in your house or room, say, "I don't smoke and it does bother me." You have not criticized them, nor have you given them a lecture on smoking (they have heard plenty)—you just expressed your own personal opinion. Acceptance says, "I may not like what you do, but I like you." When you accept them, people try to please you.

2. Teach people what is right. Sometimes people do things we don't like because they simply don't know any better. Wrong is wrong because it hurts; right is right because it works. Often people will automatically drop wrong when they can identify it.

One time I was the guest at a home where the father harshly criticized his son. He said, "You have the manners of a pig; you aren't fit to eat with normal people. Leave the table." The little boy was crushed under the cruel criticism of the father. I remembered that lesson, and I have made it a policy to call attention to the right that people do rather than the wrong. So, when my son was eating with his fingers, I said to him, "John watch me eat with the fork. It's easier, more polite, healthier, you don't have to wash your hands after dinner, and people like you better than when you eat with your fingers." I did not criticize his bad manners. I simply taught him better manners.

3. Reward good behavior and ignore the bad. A popular therapy used to change bad behavior in problem children is called behavior modification. B. F. Skinner identified a technique that is called operant conditioning. When you ignore behavior that you don't want and reward behavior that you do want, the unwanted behavior is abandoned and the reinforced behavior is continued. When animals are rewarded for doing what their trainer wants, they learn much more quickly than when they are punished for misbehavior. What is true of animals is also true of human beings. Criticism is punishment. Praise is reward. If we really want people to change, we will praise them when they improve.

Our United States economy (the best in the world) is based on the principle of rewards. We get paid for what we do, and the better we do it, the more we get paid. It would be good for management to remember that the reward of praise is also an excellent motivator. Some companies think the only way to reward performance is with money. Given a choice, some employees would be happier with a different reward like days off, recognition, or encouragement and praise.

4. Motivate people through encouragement. Criticism establishes blame and brings problem solving to a halt. Encouragement brings hope and helps the person to solve the problem. Jesus used encouragement. To His disciples He said, "Lo I am with you always, even unto the end of the world" (Matt. 28:20). To the woman caught in adultery, "Neither do I condemn thee; go, and sin no more" (John 8:11). To the paralytic, "Take heart, son; your sins are forgiven" (Matt. 9:2, NIV). Because sickness was often seen as a punishment for sin in those days, this would have been an especially encouraging word.

If at any time you are having difficulties with a loved one, try encouragement. Sometimes we take advantage of the ones we love and fall into the kind of nagging and carping that everyone except the one doing it recognizes as criticism. Instead, try speaking a word of praise and encouragement. You will be amazed at how influential you can be.

5. Pray for people and bless them. Jesus said, "Love your enemies, do good to those who hate you, bless those who curse you, pray for those who mistreat you" (Luke 6:27–28, NIV). These words are foreign to our natural tendency to love those who love us and hate those who hate us. Few people ever practice this passage, but those who do declare amazing results.

One day a deranged man threatened to kill me. He said via telephone that he had purchased a gun and would blow me away after I had suffered awhile. I thought, *Two can play at this game; I'll purchase a gun.* The man stalked and threatened me for weeks. One day when he called I said to him, "God bless you. I want you to know that I am praying for you and wish for you the best of everything." That's the last time I heard from him. Screaming back at him and threatening did not work. Prayer and blessing did.

CHECK YOUR SKILL

I taught the Dale Carnegie Course to a group of General Motors executives. The principle of the course was to never criticize—that people grow better by pointing out what they do right, rather than what they do wrong. The GM executives insisted that I break the rules and criticize them so that they would know how to improve. In fact, they complained to Mr. Carnegie, himself. So, I was instructed to point out their failings. To the first man who spoke, I said, "You need to make eye contact with your audience." He put his hands on his hips, glared at me, and said, "You're not so hot yourself." I hadn't asked for criticism; he had. Mr. Carnegie was right, "It doesn't pay to criticize."

Try this activity. Jot down the five alternatives to criticism we just discussed and carry them with you in your purse, wallet, or planner. Next time you're tempted to criticize, select one of the alternatives and practice using it instead.

CHAPTER 8

CONFRONTING
SUCCESSFULLY

When people, especially strangers, say something I disagree with, I usually keep my mouth shut. I only talk back when the issue is important.

—MY WIFE [I HAVE HER TRAINED]

One day the police knocked on our door. Our neighbor had lodged a complaint that our dog was using his yard as a restroom. After the police left, I went to see my neighbor to assure him that we would control our dog better and use a pooper-scooper. The neighbor ranted, raved, cursed, and threatened to kill me and my dog. What should have been a minor incident and a successful confrontation became a tempest in a teapot and estranged me and my neighbor. Overreaction is not a successful confrontation! Sometimes it is absolutely necessary to confront and let people know the lines of demarcation, but if we don't do it right we will stir up a storm.

I worked for a while as a clinical psychologist at Terminal Island Federal Prison. It seemed to me that the convicts and inmates had deficiencies in their ability to confront. The least little deviation was an excuse for them to go into a purple rage. Instead of politely saying something like, "The soup isn't up to its usual excellence today but has a strange taste to me," they would say, "You don't expect me to eat this bowl of sewage [or worse] do you?" Then they might curse or throw the bowl. Frequently a small incident would become a fight.

History is choked with minor confrontations escalating into major conflicts. Countries employ highly skilled ambassadors who carefully use tactful words to keep down confrontations that could lead to war among nations. I suppose that violence is sometimes unavoidable, but it is not within the scope of my recommendations. I believe in friendly, gentle, and reasonable confrontations that lead to a better understanding and relationships.

Confrontation is different from criticism in that criticism is often done in secret, like gossip. Confrontation is between two or more people, similar to a conflict in court. Criticism is a complaint against some person, institution, or event. Confrontation involves at least two people, and is an attempt to work out a difficulty. Criticism is an attack and seldom tries to work out anything.

WHAT TO DO WHEN SOMEONE CONFRONTS YOU

If someone comes to you with a confrontation, here are some things to remember:

1. Don't fuel their anger. The louder they get, the softer you get. Battles are sometimes won with loud voices and angry venom, but wars never are.

2. Listen before you respond. Find out what they have to say before you answer back. If you know what their side is, perhaps the problems will be easily absolved. People who start angry have been known to apologize at the end.

3. Calmly state your point of view. In a soft, reasonable way explain your side of the conflict, if it differs from theirs. Try to diffuse emotional reactions with an intelligent response.

4. *Agree to seek some help.* If you can't see eye to eye and it seems appropriate, ask to call in a moderator, a mutual friend, or a respected colleague. Say, "You may be right; I never thought of it before. Let's see what George has to say."

5. *Don't rush yourself.* If they don't want a moderator, then suggest, "I need a little time to think about this. I'll get back to you shortly."

6. *Try to part in a friendly way.* If you can't at the moment, then make it a point to make peace at a later time.

7. *Face up to your mistake.* Don't be afraid to admit it, and apologize if you are wrong. A big person can admit mistakes. A picayunish little person is always right—he thinks.

8. *Diplomatically handle another's mistake.* If you think that you are right, you might say, "I have thought this over, and I don't think I have done anything wrong; but I don't want to upset you or lose your friendship, so let's talk it over and reach some compromise."

9. *Be very careful and conciliatory.* Unfortunately, despite your diplomacy and care, these are days of violence where people kill at the slightest provocation.

10. *Call authorities as a last resort.* Unless violence either develops or is threatened, don't call the police.

HOW TO IMPLEMENT EFFECTIVE CONFRONTATION

Sometimes you are the one who must do the confronting. Perhaps it is your job to reprimand or fire an employee; or it becomes your task to confront a friend, relative, neighbor, or a stranger. It is not possible to endure the situation any longer, and you must do something. Here are some ways to handle it:

1. *Pray about it.* I am a firm believer in seeking the leadership of our Creator before undertaking a difficult task like confronting. Often we forget our faith and confront impulsively and tactlessly. Facing up to a person who you think has goofed up or done the wrong thing can be traumatic and,

sometimes, even dangerous. We need all the guidance we can get, and prayer is the best place to start.

Not long ago I felt constrained to write a confrontation letter to someone who I thought had stepped over the line of propriety. I earnestly prayed to God for direction, and then I consulted my pastor. I believe God used my pastor to speak to me. He said, "If you can write this letter in love with no thought of judgment or revenge, then do so." I struggled with this advice because I was angry and wanted to kick the person's behind for what he had done. It took two weeks before I could wrestle myself into the proper spirit and write a helpful, loving letter. I thank God I did.

If it is at all possible, confront a person face-to-face. Don't write a letter unless there is no other way. If you must write, do so with great care, and then get the opinion of a respected person. Letters are documented evidence. Never write one in anger.

2. Choose an appropriate time. Confrontations that come quickly, like in traffic, can be spontaneously ugly. We need to keep ourselves in such a mood that sudden fist shaking or curse words will not bring a response in kind. A sudden blast of a horn or screech of tires can fire the adrenal glands and bring instant fear or anger. We need to keep ourselves prayed up so that quick anger does not get us into quick trouble. It is always particularly disconcerting when a driver with a Jesus sign on his car cuts you off or tells you via sign language what to do. We expect better. If you have a Jesus sign, then act like Him.

3. Consider carefully one's personality and emotions. Particularly, confrontations with family members and friends need to be done with careful awareness of moods and temperament. Whenever my wife found it necessary to confront me, she would choose a time when I wasn't stressed out with other problems. With Type A people, that can be difficult. That is why I recommend a regular family hour to air difficulties and renew allegiances.

4. Begin a confrontation in a friendly way. Nothing always works; but one thing is sure: a hostile, angry beginning will almost always fail. If you must tell someone something uncomfortable, start in a friendly way—give a compliment. If you can't find anything good to say about the person, then don't bother to confront. You will lose.

One time I had a knife collection. It was just a hobby. Ralph stole my knife collection. He was the only one that could have done it. I was afraid to confront him and listen to his lies or lose a member of our church. With great reluctance I finally went to him and said, "Ralph, I see we have something in common—we both like knives. I was happy to loan my collection to you for a while, but now I'd like it back." He said OK and brought it back to me. That was a successful confrontation, and no one was offended.

5. *Be a peacemaker.* Jesus said that if anyone takes your coat, give him your cloak also (see Matt. 5:40). In other words, don't value possessions (no matter how important) more than relationships with people. When you are in the middle of a discussion, don't protect your property more than the people. Be a peacemaker, establish good relationships—then the property will be safe.

6. *Use your brains, not your emotions.* Anyone who hysterically confronts someone may win a temporary battle, but in the end they will lose. You may say how you feel about a subject and tell them you are not comfortable with the situation, but you must have a sensible, reasonable, common-sense reason for the confrontation. If justice, fair play, and common sense are not on your side and you confront, you will lose.

7. *Use the method of Jesus.*

"Moreover if thy brother shall trespass against thee, go and tell him his fault between thee and him alone: if he shall hear thee, thou hast gained thy brother. But if he will not hear thee, then take with thee one or two more, that in the mouth of two or three witnesses every word may be established. And if he shall neglect to hear them, tell it unto the church: but if he neglect to hear the church, let him be unto thee as a heathen man and a publican." (Matt. 18:15–17)

The order of confrontation is very important. Notice that Jesus recommended (1) confronting the person alone first;

(2) if it doesn't work, take some witnesses and confront again; (3) if that doesn't do it, you can tell the whole church and let them confront him; (4) if he still won't listen, then drop him—he isn't worth it.

Unfortunately, many times we skip the first three steps and start with number 4, immediately dropping him and ostracizing him. After the fact, we may go to number 3 and tell the whole wide world what a stinker he is. Seldom do we go any further and call witnesses or, heaven forbid, have a personal one-on-one conversation with the person. Because we don't follow Jesus' order, much ill will exists along with hurt feelings and estrangement.

8. Don't confront overwhelming force unless you are prepared to pay the price. To walk up to a street gang with knives, clubs, and guns and say to them, "You fellows are making too much noise; get off the street," will have dangerous repercussions for you. There is a time for confrontation, and there is a time for silence.

9. Don't have too many confrontations. Confrontations are stress inducing. We are not all born like Ralph Nader, who spends a worthwhile life confronting big business. To the ordinary person, confrontations can cause anxiety attacks and physical illness. If you are having too many confrontations, perhaps the problems are coming from you. Take some counseling sessions to explore your motivations, or consult with your pastor.

10. Remember the purpose of confrontations. It is not to make people look bad, put them down, take vengeance, or to get your own way. The purpose of confrontations is to resolve conflict and to successfully live with other people without antagonism. It is impossible to avoid some hurt in a confrontation, but don't make it permanent; bring harmony as quickly as possible to your relationships.

TAKING THE HURT
OUT OF CONFRONTATION

We have put forth ten suggestions on how to act when someone confronts you, and ten suggestions to follow when you must confront someone else. There is another vitally important ingredient in confrontations. Many times confrontations, given or received, end in bad feelings and make permanent enemies. How can we confront without hurting or being hurt?

Be careful. No matter how much care you use in confronting people, even minor problems can escalate into fracture. One time I drove quite a few miles to visit one of my sons. I suppose it was bad timing and he was stressed out, but he didn't greet me with a hug or a warm hello. Furthermore, during the week I was there he didn't bother to sit down and have a friendly chat. I was crushed. Am I more sensitive than most people? I think not. It cannot be emphasized too much how easy it is to hurt people. It could have taken me six months to get over my bruised feelings, but I went directly to him, looked him in the eye, and told him how I felt. He replied, "I'm sorry, I'm just preoccupied with opening a new business." We are now at peace. If a confrontation is forced upon you, do it very carefully, but do it.

Confront yourself first. Many times when we feel the need to censure someone for their conduct, a close look will reveal that we are guilty of the same thing ourselves. Jesus said very plainly, "Why do you look at the speck of sawdust in your brother's eye and pay no attention to the plank in your own eye? How can you say to your brother, 'Let me take the speck out of your eye,' when all the time there is a plank in your own eye? You hypocrite, first take the plank out of your own eye, and then you will see clearly to remove the speck from your brother's eye" (Matt. 7:3–5, NIV).

How can it be said any better? Human beings have impulses to resolve their guilt by censuring others for their own crimes. When you confront to relieve your own guilt, it is particularly offensive to others.

Balance negative with positive. Scratches on a Rolls Royce are so much easier to yell about than the work on a beautifully polished car is to rave about. When we choose to confront someone because we are bothered about what they do or say, we must take some time to exclaim about the positive, not the negative. I have heard many people say, "After all I did for him," or "I worked like a slave, and he noticed only one little flaw." How easy it is to search for flaws and to seek offense, just as we notice a tiny run in the stocking of a beautifully dressed woman. Only when the negative becomes oppressive—and the other person can do something about it—should we confront.

Confront the problem, not the person. The Old Testament teaches us that God hates sin. The New Testament teaches us that God loves sinners. We would be wise to do both—love the sinner, but hate the sin. People have a fragile self-esteem based upon how people evaluate them. That is particularly true of the young who are so sensitive to their peer group. It is easy to damage them in trying to solve a minor problem.

Do not confront by jumping all over the person and calling him names. Words like "you stupid jerk" or "you [expletive, expletive]" do not make a successful confrontation; rather, it is an assault. How about, "I like you, Joe [or I love you, Mary], but we need to work out a problem. Let's talk about it." Don't smash at an ego; confront a problem.

Use "I think," rather than "you are." In learning how to confront other people without hurting them, we need to be very careful in using certain words like *you, must, shouldn't, always,* and *never. You* is an attack, *must* is a command, *shouldn't* is a guilt trip, and *always* and *never* are absolutes. Instead of saying, "You are driving too fast," say, "I don't like fast driving." The word *I* is emphasized, rather than the personal word *you.*

When we say, "You are a liar," we are making a personal attack that can only end in the person being defensive and launching a counterattack. Try saying, "I have a hard time thinking that way," or "I see things differently," or any combination of words that changes the emphasis from *you* to *I.* We are not out to get a person, we are out to change a behavior.

Don't just confront—provide help. It is easy to point out what another person is doing wrong. It is much more difficult to do it right yourself. During World War II a master sergeant had trained thousands of men on the proper way to get down quickly by falling on your rifle. He finally went to combat and was killed when he didn't get down quickly enough. It's one thing to teach; it's another thing to do. When we confront people for their inadequacies, we need to put ourselves in their place. Their job may not be as easy as we think.

This is a plea for sympathy and patience. Remember that when we have been doing something for twenty years, the other person may not be able to master it in twenty minutes.

Confront in love. Confrontation can be quite toxic, particularly when accompanied by bitterness and resentment, so confront in love.

When we point out another person's failings in a derogatory way, that's not love. When we put another person down in a personal attack, that's not love. When we reject a person with an ugly verbal attack, that's not love. When we make another person the object of a cruel joke or ridicule, that's not love. Well, what is love? Let me quote from 1 Corinthians 13:

> Love is patient, love is kind. It does not envy, it does not boast, it is not proud. It is not rude, it is not self-seeking, it is not easily angered, it keeps no record of wrongs. Love does not delight in evil but rejoices with the truth. It always protects, always trusts, always hopes, always perseveres. (vv. 4–7, NIV)

Because I know that God loves me with this kind of love, I am able to show this love to others. It doesn't mean that I will never confront. Jesus confronted, very strongly; so did the apostle Paul. We must remember that we won't always make friends or change people through confrontation. But to the best of our ability, we must strive to confront without causing unnecessary pain.

CHECK YOUR SKILL

Pick one hour of primetime TV and observe how the characters handle confrontation. Make a scorecard containing the principles in this chapter and note the number of times each principle is used or violated. If you have older children, make this a family learning activity.

CHAPTER 9

LEADING AND FOLLOWING

He didn't get along with people; they had to get along with him. He kowtowed to the people above him, and bullied those below.

—SAID ABOUT GEORGE PATTON

When we were little kids playing sandlot baseball, we would choose two captains who then selected his or her team from those remaining. I was always the last one chosen, and I could expect either leader to say, "Do we have to get stuck with him?" Since I was physically handicapped, no one wanted me to be on their side in a baseball game. However, I was not mentally handicapped, and I would be one of the first ones selected in a spelling bee contest. I was not a leader and was not even considered a good follower in baseball. That's what makes me qualified to write this chapter on leading and following—I have both failed and succeeded all through my life.

It has been said that some people are born leaders and others are followers. There may be some inborn genetic tendencies, but I think leaders and followers are made by the call of the situation. Moses was a meek man, yet he led the children of Israel to great heights. Timing and the call of God made him a leader. King David as a young man was considered to be so unpromising as a leader that his father did not even mention him when the prophet came to anoint the one God had chosen to become king.

QUALITIES OF A LEADER

What people skills must one have to be selected as a good leader?

A GOOD LEADER
SHARES THE SPOTLIGHT

Not being able to delegate authority is the quickest way to destroy a good leader. One who inspires to lead must have someone to direct. Without followers, where is leadership? The leader, whether president, king, or scout master, needs people and so must master people skills. Good leaders readily give their followers credit for successes. Ineffective leaders hog the spotlight for themselves.

A GOOD LEADER HAS
A GOOD PERSONALITY

Developing charisma, an attractive personality, will not ensure a good following, but almost everything we do to improve will help. Some characteristics are self-evident:

- a healthy body in good condition from vigorous exercise, work, and active recreation
- appropriate grooming in which the most important factor is keeping yourself clean
- a pleasant personality with which you can smile, laugh, joke, and play in a friendly way
- a love of and compassion for people
- good ethical concepts which includes a respect for the rules of our society
- a strong commitment to a good cause

- an ability to make competent decisions
- a friendly relationship to a loving God

If you are working on improving yourself, you are doing well.

A GOOD LEADER HAS SOME DEGREE OF COMPETENCE

The rule is rather simple: If you want to be a good follower or leader on a team, then you certainly must develop competence. Competence is the number one way to develop confidence, and it can be called the way to the top. That's what Zig Ziglar says in his book *See You at the Top*. As *yes* without *no* has no meaning, so confidence without competence is worthless. It is imperative to develop at least one talent in which we become highly qualified.

A GOOD LEADER HAS CONFIDENCE IN SELF

Self-confidence has become an overworked concept in our society, especially when it is taught as an attitude of mind with no reference to ability. Self-confidence grows out of some successful experiences or at least some hope of them coming to pass. Belief in ourselves, coupled with belief in the people around us, depends largely on faith in God.

I went to the funeral of a fine thirteen-year-old boy. He had been praised liberally and had developed a high degree of self-confidence—which is very good. But he thought he could do anything, so he took the family car for a final spin. Belief in self must be coupled with reality.

Confidence comes from a developing talent, some successful experiences, reasonable thinking, belief in our fellow passengers in life, and a profound faith in God.

A GOOD LEADER HAS A MAGNIFICENT OBSESSION

A great cause will create great leaders. Who ever heard of Dwight Eisenhower before World War II, or Norman

Schwarzkopf and Colin Powell before Desert Storm? Thousands of leaders come to the forefront because they have a magnificent obsession, or a crisis event has come about. Emergency turns on the green light that brings leaders from the ranks. Even in times of peace we select our leaders by rigorously testing them through the ranks.

A GOOD LEADER IS CONSISTENT
AND A STRONG DECISION-MAKER

If an umpire in a baseball game were to call the runner out and then say, "I've changed my mind; he's safe;" the umpire would be "out." Right or wrong, a leader must decide and consistently stick with it. In fact, great leaders are stubbornly persistent. Waffling will weaken a leader in ways that a wrong decision will not. Adolf Hitler was still in power after he made the disastrous mistake of invading Russia. Our democratic leaders are allowed to change their minds, but it weakens them.

A GOOD LEADER IS ABLE TO FACE
OPPOSITION AND TAKE CRITICISM

A famous quote comes from President Harry Truman: "If you can't take the heat, get out of the kitchen." Remember the opposition the Son of God had to take from the religious rulers of His day. Jesus said, "If they have called the master of the house Beelzebub, how much more shall they call them of his household?" (Matt. 10:25). No one—that means absolutely no one—can do anything of importance without making enemies and generating conflict. You can also expect that your enemies will get organized to fight you, so be brave and courageous. Take up your cross and follow Him.

A GOOD LEADER INSPIRES
CONFIDENCE AND REWARDS PEOPLE

An army needs a supply of food and clothing, plus weapons and rest. If a leader does not supply the necessary equipment, he will lose his army. Also the leader must furnish esprit d' corps without which the army cannot fight, and may even run away. Any leader in the business world, sports, family, or church does well to consider the needs of his followers, give them their rewards, and inspire confidence.

TRUST: THE KEY TO
LEADING AND FOLLOWING

Recently, an organization of Christian men called Promise Keepers has held large, successful meetings across our land. It's about time someone emphasized keeping promises. Our divorce rate is astronomical from broken promises; and when parents break promises to their children, the children lose faith in people. The importance of keeping promises, how to strengthen resolve, and how to encourage others to keep their promises deserves to occupy our attention.

A man or a woman, a boy or a girl, any person of any age can have all the virtues of heaven bestowed upon them, but if a word is broken and a promise is not kept, virtue flies out the window. All relationships—God to people and people to people—depend upon faith, and faith depends upon keeping a promise. Don't promise God anything unless you intend to keep your promise. In fact, don't promise anything even to your pet dog, unless you intend to keep your promise. My dad promised me that when I got out of the hospital he would take me for a ride in his speedboat, "Barnacle Bill." He kept me alive with that promise, but he devastated me when he didn't keep it. Not long ago a friend invited me to the coast to take his boat out into the ocean and go salmon fishing. I drove five hundred miles for that boat ride. When I got there—no ride, no fishing trip—just a lot of empty excuses awaited me. It reminded me of past broken promises and made me struggle hard to maintain my faith in that person.

Recently, a couple came to see me. They had been married for eight years, had two children, a new car, a lovely home, and good, secure jobs. The young man said to me, "I'm not attracted to my wife anymore. I want a divorce; I want to be free to explore the field."

His wife said, "You are already exploring the field. What can I do to win you back? Think of our home and children. We will lose everything."

I interrupted, "I was at your beautiful wedding eight years ago at a prestigious church with three hundred guests and three pastors. You promised to 'have and to hold, from this day forward, for better for worse, for richer for poorer, in sickness and in health, to love and to cherish, till death do us part.' What happened to your promise?"

He flippantly replied, "I don't feel like keeping it anymore."

What a tragedy for that man's children, his wife, his church, his community, and most all for him. When we break our promises, we will no longer be the leaders of our families; and at the very least, we will grieve the heart of God. How can God honor such a life? And I'm sorry, but I just don't buy the phony excuses like "I don't feel like it" or "Everybody does it, so it's OK."

In the blockbuster movie *Forrest Gump*, Forrest promises his friend Bubba that they will be partners in the shrimp business and later gives half his earnings to Bubba's mother. The poor woman is so shocked when Gump keeps his promise that she passes out on her front porch. Of course, that's only a movie. Not all of us in real life are as honorable as Gump. Breaking promises is so common that many of us have become cynical and accept it as part of life. Politicians especially seem to know how hard it is to keep promises.

Pete Wilson, governor of California, had promised that if elected governor he would not run for president, but he did—even if for only a brief time. In a poll, 59 percent of Californians said they disapproved of a Wilson presidential run.

During his 1992 campaign for president, then Arkansas Governor Bill Clinton promised that, if he were elected president, he would cut taxes for the middle class. He raised taxes.

When seeking the GOP presidential nomination, Vice-President George Bush told the Republican convention in August 1988: "Read my lips; no new taxes." In 1990, he agreed to a $134 billion tax increase.

"I promise I'll always love you."

"I promise I'll pay you back."

"I won't tell anybody, I promise."

We could go on and on with examples of promise breaking, but that would be discouraging. Promises are mostly kept every day. Husbands and wives honor their promises to each other, employees put in an honest day's work, and yes, even politicians keep *some* of their promises. Many people go out of their way to fulfill their commitments.

Judy Collins is a clerk working in California state government. Several years ago, she and her husband, David, promised her mother that they would care for her when she became ill. They took care of her in their Sacramento home for more than five years. She died after having a stroke last spring.

"It was very difficult," Judy said. "I had to take time off from work, and it put a strain on the entire family, but I'm really glad that we did it. I felt that I honored my promise to my mother, and my children saw that promises mean something."

A promise is a commitment. It shouldn't be taken lightly. Maybe we should think twice before we make too many promises. Jesus said, "Let your Yes be 'Yes,' and your 'No,' 'No'" (Matt. 5:37, NKJV).

CHECK YOUR SKILL

Read the marks of a good leader below (as compiled by Herbert J. Taylor). Rate yourself from one to ten (with one being never and ten being all the time) on the frequency you practice these traits. Highlight your three strongest qualities.

TEN MARKS OF A GOOD LEADER

1. He is well informed on local and world affairs. "Knowledge is the food of the soul" (Plato).

2. He is courteous, unselfish, friendly—gets along well with others—is a good neighbor. "All is well with him who is beloved by his neighbors" (George Herbert).

3. He is sincere, dependable, and takes an active part in the church. "Religion is the basis of civil society" (Edmund Burke).

4. He appreciates what others have done for him and accepts responsibility for the future betterment of his community. "A community is like a ship; everyone ought to be prepared to take the helm" (Henrik Ibsen).

5. He is fair and just in his relations with others. "Hear the other side" (Augustine).

6. He obeys the laws of his community, his God, and his nation. "No man is above the law" (Theodore Roosevelt).

7. He votes regularly and intelligently at election time. "The greatest menace to freedom is an inert people" (Louis D. Brandeis).

8. He is interested in the freedom and welfare of all the world's peoples and does his part to secure them. "Slav, Teuton, Celt, I count them all my friends and brother souls" (Tennyson).

9. He is productive—renders a worthwhile service to his fellow man. "The highest of distinctions is service to others" (King George VI).

10. He sets a good example to the youth of his community. "A good example is the best sermon" (Thomas Fuller).

A good leader must first of all be a good follower. When a man or woman submits to the authority of God, he or she has taken the first step in the prerequisites of leadership. Who wants a leader that has no understanding of what it means to follow or to submit.

A Bag of Tools

Isn't it strange
That princes and kings,
And clowns that caper
In sawdust rings,
And common people
Like you and me
Are builders for eternity?

Each is given a bag of tools,
A shapeless mass,
A book of rules;
And each must make,
Ere life is flown,
A stumbling block
Or a stepping-stone.

—R. L. Sharpe

CHAPTER 10

LISTENING

No one is useless in this world who lightens the burden of it to anyone else.

—CHARLES DICKENS

A lot of the trouble in this world stems from people who refuse to listen. They don't listen to their friends, to nature, to science, to the still small voice, or to the loud clear voice. They don't listen even to their own bodies. People don't listen and so they pay the consequences. To listen effectively is a marvelous skill and can be life changing to anyone who listens or is fortunate enough to be listened to.

We often wonder why God does not have more to say about our life and its circumstances. Perhaps God wonders why we do not listen to the many messages for our benefit that He is trying to communicate. God says, "[You] have ears to hear, and you hear not" (Ezek. 12:2). Perhaps those who read the following pages may become better listeners and hence get along with people better, have an abundant life more easily available, and find the promise of eternity more firmly established.

The average person listens interruptively. That is, he holds a thought while the other person is talking. As soon as he can find a breath break, he interrupts with his own idea. These people never know what anyone is saying; they just want to express themselves. It is actually comical when two interrupters get together to fight for the stage.

THE BENEFITS OF GOOD LISTENING

Why should we listen to anyone? We are independent, free people and we do what we want to do.

"Stop! You're going to walk over the cliff!" you exclaim.

"Why should I listen to you?" I say on the way down.

We listen because listening expands our ears and our eyes and makes us aware through the voice of other people of much broader aspects of life.

LISTENING KEEPS US SAFE

We listen to save ourselves from getting hurt by falling over the cliff. We listen to the growl of a bear, to the hiss of a snake, to the snarl of a wolf—all to save ourselves from getting hurt. We listen to the sounds of nature: the churning of the wind, the rumble of thunder, the crash of rocks in an avalanche, and the shaking of our shelter in an earthquake. We listen because if we didn't listen, we would not be secure in a threatening world.

WE CAN AVOID THE
MISTAKES OF THE PAST

At times people rebel against authority—parents, peer groups, and society—both superior and inferior ones. Those who do not listen are doomed to repeat the crippling mistakes of everyone they meet. Those who do not listen to the voice of history will find themselves reliving a stupidity that a distant relative learned five thousand years ago. Rebels may feel free, but they are in the greatest prison of all. Their prison is having to learn everything from ground zero all by themselves.

LISTENING IS GOOD THERAPY

Another benefit of listening is that it helps people who need to talk. Good listening is therapy. Here's how therapy works. A person has a problem. There are four things they need to know:

1. What the problem might be. Some people can think out answers in their head. Other people do not know what they are thinking until they hear what they are saying. Talking out their problem is one way of constructing a clear view of what that problem is.

2. Just talking is not enough. Someone else must listen with understanding so that two minds are engaged in discovering the nature of the problem—where it came from and what caused it.

3. Explore and discuss possible solutions to the problems.

4. Formulate a solution and take action on it. Talking and listening need to be followed up by a program of action. Problem solving consists of identification, causation, solutions, and action; this involves thinking, emoting, talking, listening, and feedback.

LISTENING INCREASES LEARNING

Good listeners learn more and do so more quickly than bad listeners. Good listeners are safer and more secure because they hear warning messages. Good listeners are happier than bad listeners because they know the rules. Good listeners accomplish more in life because they have more input. Good listeners can help other people because they know how. Good listeners have a most important people skill.

I stopped at a store in Montana that sold ice. After I fumbled around for a little while, I read the large sign on the side of the ice house door right in front of me: "When all else fails, try reading the instructions." Poor listeners do not read the instructions; hence, they can neither get propane or blocks of ice or anything else that requires an explanation.

One of the favorite sayings my parents interjected upon me as a child was, "Children are to be seen and not heard." I didn't think that saying was fair when I was a child, so as a parent I never used it. I believe that we should listen to every voice long enough to inspect whether or not it is for us before we turn it off. I have very good kids, in part because I believed they should be both seen and heard.

LISTENING BETWEEN THE LINES

Listening is an art. Like any art, though, we begin with basic skills. Often we listen, not to what is being said, but to our own noise, to our own sound. Even when our body is speaking to us loud and clear, we do not hear what it is saying unless we cultivate the skill of listening.

The good listener listens between the lines, which requires a number of techniques:

First, developing the art of listening requires the use of *discipline*. A thousand monkeys pounding on a thousand pianos in a random way will never by accident come up with one of the symphonies of Beethoven. It takes disciplined learning, not random pounding, to produce good music. It also takes disciplined listening, not unfocused hearing, to produce a person who knows what is being said.

Second, a good listener learns how to *concentrate*. We do a number of things at the same time and screen out all extraneous messages. To listen well we must focus our attention. By concentrating intensely, we open our ears to the stimuli that is meant for us. We must give our full attention to the situation at hand. The good listener needs an open mind, but not so open that it fails to screen the nonconsequential. If we do not concentrate, screen, and focus, then it will be done for us, and some voice that has no message will captivate our brains.

Third, a good listener seeks to *comprehend* the true meaning of what is being said. My children sometimes said, "I hate you." What did they mean? They felt frustrated, directed, and controlled. Almost everyone gets angry occasionally at over-directive parents.

However, *I hate you* does not always mean "I hate you." It probably just means, "You are bugging me right now." We are not good listeners if we give a literal translation to every word spoken. Remember that people are often careless with their speech. Listen carefully to comprehend what the communicator is really communicating. Don't listen with prejudice, condemnation, or criticism. Listen for meaning.

Fourth, comprehension has the added ingredient of being able to *recall* some sampling of what has been read or heard. Recall is based upon three fundamental principles: fixation, repetition, and pairing. *Fixation* simply means the amount of attention you pay to the message. *Repetition* consists of going over the meaning until we can remember it. *Pairing* means to associate the message to the events of life. A message that has no meaning to us can't fix itself, will not be remembered, and can find no application.

Fifth, in order for a message to have meaning, it must find a place within the *context* of the speaker. I remember one time experiencing a severe earthquake. My little boy asked me what caused earthquakes. I began an elaborate explanation of tectonic plates and the movement of earth faults. My little boy looked at me and said, "That's not how earthquakes are caused. A giant grabs hold of a tall tree and pulls it back and forth." My little boy was ready for that explanation but not ready for earth faults.

Sixth, consider different *languages* and inflections in the use of words to convey meaning. If we don't know the language the speaker is using, we get little of his meaning. If the speaker is talking too low or too loud, using slang, sarcasm, idioms or any nuance of words, sometimes we miss the meaning. When we are prejudiced and have preconceived ideas, we put words and ideas into the speaker's mouth and that isn't sanitary.

Seventh, *two people* are involved in listening. One is the person who is talking, and the other is the person who is listening. In a good conversation where communication is involved, rarely does one person listen all the time or one person talk all the time. We take turns. On occasions some people need to talk a lot which forces us to listen a lot. When a person needs to talk and

we don't want to listen, we can do a lot of damage. Most psychotherapy is talk therapy. A person is full of poisonous ideas, and
they talk them out to an empathetic listener. There is much
value for a "need to" talker to find someone who will listen.

You can get some idea of what level of stress or distress the
person is experiencing when you watch for the physiological
signs: dilated pupils, cold or sweaty hands, trembling, nervous
tics, undue emotionality, poor balance, or untidy appearance.
When you listen to what makes a person laugh or cry and
what they keep talking about, you can pick up inconsistencies
and attempts at deception.

A lot of people get so depressed that they become determined to commit suicide. I have talked many people out of
their determination to die. Interestingly enough, I didn't talk
so much as I "listened" them out of the idea.

LISTENING TO PEOPLE
WHO NEED TO TALK

There are a number of important principles to remember
when listening to people who need to talk.

Let them know that you are listening. You can do this by nod-
ding your head to certain provocative remarks or saying small
awareness noises, such as "uh-huh," "yes," "I hear you," "my-
my," or any other such feedback that lets the other person know
that you are listening. It is particularly important when listening
to a person on the telephone to let them know that you are still
there. Who has not had the experience of talking and suddenly
becoming aware that you have been cut off and not knowing
when it happened. Every several sentences you must reassure a
"need to" talker that you are listening. If they ever get the idea
that you are not listening, all communication stops.

Interject an occasional question for clarification. Say to the person: "Did I hear you say . . ." or "Did you mean . . ." or "Let
me see if I understand you. I heard you say . . ." Again the
exact interjection is not so important as the idea of getting the
other person's meaning. Often a "need to" talker knows what

he wants to say inside, but he fails to put it together in cogent, clear terms. Do not be afraid to ask people to repeat what they said, or to put it in your own words and ask them if that is what they said. Clarification questions are a necessary part of good communication, particularly with a person who wants you to understand how he feels.

Many times people either talk too fast or are so confused, inconsistent, or unclear that it requires a lot of intervention to get their story straight. One good way to clarify what people are saying is to make them talk slower as you write it down. This rule particularly applies to the "need to" talkers who often spill out much information so fast that it is difficult to remember it unless you write it down.

Give appropriate responses. For example, if the person says, "My mother died last Tuesday," and you laugh and say, "How funny!" you have just lost the benefit the person might receive from you. If the other person says: "My wife just ran away with a salesman," and you respond, "I've got some things I'd like to sell to her," you might as well move immediately to Tasmania. The Bible encourages us to weep with those who weep, and rejoice with those who rejoice. In other words, match the emotion of the person who is talking to you.

Maintain the trappings of good listening. These include eye contact, a semi-intelligent expression on your face, no yawning or drooping eyelids, evidence of alertness, and a certain amount of compassionate ambiance that lets the other person know by your facial expressions and your attentiveness that you are listening to them.

Keep your mind in gear. Make intelligent remarks to the person's story. I was watching a counselor through a one-way glass one day during a training session. The woman told the counselor about her husband and children, and she complained vociferously about the indifferent treatment that her husband gave to her. After five minutes, the counselor responded, "Are you married?" Of course the woman knew immediately that the counselor had not listened to a word she had said. If a person needs to talk, you need to avoid stupid remarks that let him or her know you were in dreamland and not listening.

If you listen to a person and find your mind wandering, either excuse yourself and go to the restroom to splash cold water in your face, or tell the person that you aren't the right one to hear what he has to say. If you can't listen to what he has to say, you aren't the right one. Listening is a difficult discipline that requires lots of strength and energy. Self-absorbed people can rarely listen to anyone. They are so occupied with themselves that they have no time to care for anyone else.

WHEN NOT TO LISTEN

Some sounds are for me, and I must listen to them. Other noises are not for me, and I should screen them out. For example, the Bible tells us that we must not listen to the idle chatter of our servants, lest we hear them say something very detrimental about us. There are a number of voices that should not be heard.

1. Don't listen to words spoken in anger. Often they mean just the opposite of what is being said.

2. Don't take too seriously the words of someone trying to sell you something. The more that is in it for the other person, the more likely they are to throw you a curve.

3. Don't listen to people who are trying to seduce you. Some people think only of their own benefits, not yours. If you want to be seduced, that's your business, but when someone talks you into doing what you don't want to do, that hurts.

4. Screen out too much noise. It will cause stress, and stress will cause death.

5. Screen out bad words. False words, ugly words, and obscene words are all words meant to hurt and destroy. Some things *can* be heard without being reacted to.

6. Learn how to listen for the truth. You need to pluck out the error like a gardener prunes dead branches from a tree.

7. Don't listen to the negative. Put-downs and pessimistic bitter words will depress and discourage. Don't let yourself be programmed by them.

8. Don't let the devil deceive you. He doesn't talk for God, but do listen to your enemies. Enemies often speak a profound truth that no one else has the guts to utter. Listen to an enemy with caution and weigh carefully what he has to say. Don't let him get to your soft, unprotected visceral until you have had an opportunity to screen his words.

TURNING OFF UNWELCOME CHATTER

Letting people talk can be helpful; sometimes it even saves lives. Some people have a loneliness factor in which endless chatter like monkeys in a tree becomes their only means of intimacy. Their constant repetition, redundancy, and nonsensical chatter is enough to drive a person crazy. All people have occasions in which they develop diarrhea of the mouth. The ideas within have become a toxic poison, and they scatter their cancerous words to afflict any ear that will hear. A person who endures too much bad talking can program himself to be quite bitter at the endless negativisms and "ain't it awful's" of the diseased talkers. If you are cornered by one of these who must spew the air with their wicked drivel, I suggest the following:

1. Negative people want to bring you down to their level. Don't go. Remember, if you listen to too many conspiracy theories, "terrible's", and malicious gossip, it will gradually recondition you to be like they are. Bad words will make a situation bad no matter how good it starts out to be. You can stop negative people without using negative weapons, raising your voice, or lashing out in anger.

2. Don't be afraid to tell people who are repeating the same old story for the fifth time, "You've told that to me before." When you are visiting someone and they keep repeating, try saying, "I'm sorry. I'm tired of talking. I need a little rest. Could we play a game or sit quietly for a while or watch TV?" We are not doing anyone a favor, including ourselves, when we allow them to turn words into cheap, trite, and repetitive ideas.

3. When people are telling jokes that make us uncomfortable, or they are bombarding us with words we don't want to hear and ideas that we have not included in our ethical

system, it is appropriate to tell them that what they are saying offends our sensitivities. Do it first with good cheer. If they do not respond and continue the smut, then we can use reinforcement of the emotion of anger or, even better, the punishment of isolation. In any case it is important for us not to be subjected to upsetting verbalizations.

4. Sometimes people question and pry and seek to invade our privacy for the purpose of gossip or doing us harm. Even traitors and criminals on trial can plead the fifth amendment. You can say, "I don't wish to talk about this subject." If you are angry enough, you can say, "That's none of your business" or "I don't consider that question to be proper for public discussion."

I remember being in a group of men and one man asked another, "How often to you make love to your wife?" The man just looked at him and didn't say a word. His persecutor continued, getting more and more clamorous for an answer. The grieved one handled it as if he couldn't hear and pretended that the questioner was not speaking. Before long, several men in the group spoke up and said, "You're out of line." I think that not answering certain questions by acting as if you can't hear them is not a bad method of stopping the rude.

As a clinical psychologist I got paid a salary for intelligently listening to people. Psychotherapy can be described in very complex terms; but, basically, it is listening: listening with your ears, listening with the intuitive ear, listening with your eyes, listening with your mind, and listening with your emotions. Listening with your whole experiential being means that you will know and have understanding as to what is being said.

CHECK YOUR SKILLS

Mark your place in this book. Now spend one minute—wherever you are—listening actively to the sounds around you. How many of those sounds had you blocked out while you were reading?

Enlist a partner and practice the people skill of cutting out someone's annoying chatter.

CHAPTER 11

PERSUADING WITHOUT MANIPULATING

Get the other person's point of view and see things from his angle as well as your own.

—HENRY FORD

As I was writing this chapter on persuading without manipulation, I asked a number of people to review it. One person said, "I have been honing my manipulation skills all my life. Are you telling me that I have to give up my tricky methods of handling my husband?" No, I am saying there are many honest methods of persuading people to do the right thing without deceiving them. As a psychologist I have talked people out of suicide, murder, unfaithfulness, and fraud. People can be persuaded to change from the lowest to the highest or to almost anything if you know what to say and when to say it.

Persuasion is an ethical way of influencing the mind by reasons or arguments offered. We can use any method (as long as it is ethical, moral, and not self-serving) that moves the mind or passions or inclines the will to a determination. Persuasion is changing another person's mind through the use of ethical, reasonable, intelligent thought processes.

Manipulation means to control, manage, or play upon another person by artful, unfair, or insidious means, especially to one's own advantage. Motivation is a significant factor in the difference between persuasion and manipulation. If the change is all for you—that's selfish and can be labeled *manipulation*. If the change will benefit the other person, even if you do get some advantage—that's *persuasion*.

Here are some of the methods of manipulation:

1. Think only of what you want.

2. Have no sympathy.

3. Keep yourself focused on how much money you will make.

4. Capitalize on the other person's weakness.

5. If a contract is involved, be careful to hide the stingers.

6. Have no empathy; that other person is your pigeon to be used.

7. When you have taken the sucker, disappear.

A manipulator is essentially a crook, a con man who tries to take advantage of the other person in any way possible. Illegal ways number in the thousands, but in the long run none of them work.

The techniques of persuasion are not codified, nor is there much research in the field. High-talking people seem to invent their methods with ease. Low talkers are often smothered and not heard by dominant high talkers. However, the quality of speech will eventually win over the quantity. It's not how much you talk, but how reasonable the argument.

Here are a few suggestions that will assist you in persuading people to do things, and not submit them to dehumanizing manipulation.

BE NICE

Patrick Swayze played the role of a bouncer in the movie *Roadhouse*. I am not recommending the movie, but I am recommending the advice. In one scene he is instructing the other bouncers, who have had lots of mean fights. He says, "If you must ask a person to leave, be nice." When trying to persuade someone to do something, be nice. You don't need to manipulate. Being nice is just one of the many ways you can persuade people to do what you want.

My wife and I went to the beach on a very hot day. The traffic was horrendous, bumper to bumper, blocked for miles. I was trying to make a right-hand turn from a left-hand lane. In order to do that, someone had to stop and let me through. I lowered the right-hand window and asked the man in the lane next to me to let me get in front of him. He became very angry, cursed at me, and threatened to get out of the car to beat me up. His nasty response to my polite request provoked me. A hot, sweaty day with lots of nasty and angry people is a surefire formula for accidents. When people ask a favor and it really doesn't hurt you (I wasn't trying to get ahead of the man, just trying to make a turn in front of him), why not be polite? Be nice! The world will be a happier place, and there will be fewer accidents.

After fifty years of marriage counseling, I think I could sum up the greatest problem of getting along in marriage as having a bad disposition. Where do people get the idea that they can get their own way by being cranky and mean? It is OK to be firm. In fact all relationships, even the best, require firmness, confrontation, and settling differences of opinion in a pleasant way. If you want your marriage, your friendships, or your business to last and grow and be happy, then be nice.

When our granddaughter, Katie, was three years old, we had the privilege of taking care of her for awhile. She got into the medicine cabinet and swallowed fifty aspirin. We rushed her to the hospital emergency room and the doctor pumped her stomach. When she got back home, she acted as if the event was a game in which she was the center of attention. I called the child's mother, my daughter, whom I have never spanked, and asked for permission to spank my granddaughter. She responded, "Yes, if you can be nice."

I called my granddaughter to me, explained what she had done, that it might have killed her, and that she had made us very unhappy. I thought she deserved to be spanked, and her mother had given me permission. She agreed. So, I had her bend over my lap, I placed the back of my left hand against her bottom, and I proceeded to whack the palm of my left hand with the palm of my right hand. I cried out with every loud whack. It made a lot of noise, but it did not hurt her. After the sixth whack, she straightened up, looked me in the eye and said, "Stop hurting yourself, Grandpa. I won't do it again." That's one example of being nice, even when you administer a spanking.

I am not recommending corporal punishment by sharing the above example. I am simply recommending being as nice as possible when you try to persuade people to do anything.

The general overall rule of persuasion is to be nice, but there are some other suggestions.

DON'T OVERPERSUADE

As a pastor I tried hard to persuade our young people to go to summer church camp. One day I marshaled all my energy to persuade the parents of a delinquent boy to send him to summer camp. I felt it would change his life. The boy got injured when he disobeyed camp rules, and the counselors sent him home. "You were overzealous," the church board said to me, "and now it is all our fault; we have to pay the bill." When you overpersuade, you are trying to manipulate; and when you manipulate, you must bear the responsibility for what might happen. Give people the freedom to say no. When you overpower a weaker spirit, you are trying to play God and take away the power of choice.

High-pressure sales people make others fall for their hype even when they don't like the product. In the long run, beating a person down through sales pressure methods will work against the company and the product. Someone once said, "A man convinced against his will is of the same opinion still."

The FBI figures that $1.5 billion is lost each year to con artists who talk people out of their money (mostly old people) with a variety of deceitful schemes. Lies and smooth manipulation are used to sell everything from "gold bricks" to worthless mining stock to the Brooklyn bridge. Fraudulent people manipulate. Honest people persuade.

SEE THINGS FROM THE OTHER PERSON'S VIEWPOINT

Do you want to be deceived, lied to, and defrauded? No! Then resolve to treat people like you want to be treated. Ask yourself, "Why am I trying to persuade this person?" List the reasons. If all the reasons benefit you and none will benefit the other person, then you are manipulating. Stop it. It's dishonest. If in your list of reasons to persuade you find some healthy benefits for the other person and some for yourself, then go ahead. Only if it sincerely benefits the other person are you free to talk him or her into involvement.

The great Bonneville Dam on the Columbia River between Oregon and Washington had just been completed. The engineers had designed some ingenious fish ladders so the salmon could go up the river to the spawning tributaries. The only problem: the fish would not use the ladders. One engineer suggested, "We need to see things from the fish's viewpoint." The ladders were too exposed. They put baffles up to hide the fish from their predators, and the salmon resumed their run.

When we consider other persons, we will design what they want, not what we want. What man would design and build a house without consulting the wishes and desires of his wife. Instead of forcing our will and opinion on other people, we need to consider how they see things. I like nice four-door family sedans. My children like sports cars. How long would it take me to persuade them to get a sedan? Why try? Think of things from the other person's point of view and save yourself from the futility of going against personal preferences.

APPEAL TO HIGH AND NOBLE MOTIVATIONS

If someone is using powers of persuasion to talk another person into immoral or illegal behavior, the very fact that the goal is bad turns persuasion into manipulation. Talk people into doing the right thing, and they will be grateful to you. Talk people into criminal behavior, and, in the end, you are the criminal.

In a group meeting a member queried, "What would you do if God asked you to violate your conscience?" The group discussed it for awhile and reached the conclusion that God would not ask us to do the wrong thing. That's the devil's job. God is always trying to persuade us to do right.

I believe that life works out better when we are filled with love, joy, peace, patience, kindness, goodness, faithfulness, gentleness, and self-control. We pay some terrible consequences when we choose a life devoid of virtue. We will have a much easier and happier life when we appeal to basic goodness.

BE INTELLIGENT

When we feel strongly about something that involves people, we must engage our cognitive powers. Use realistic logic and reason. Controlling people with wild emotional bursts almost always fails, unless we put reasonable thoughts behind it.

We persuade people with our emotions led by our intellect. Let your intellect guide your emotions. Do not be swept away with feelings. Emotions can and do lead you to unhappiness if not controlled.

APPEAL TO THE EMOTIONS

Educators have been using IQ tests in schools for years to determine intelligence and placement in grades. There is some correlation between high intelligence and achievement but it isn't 100 percent. Some students with mediocre IQs have high achievement, and some with a genius rating fail in life. A new factor is being considered: EQ or emotional quotient. EQ is like a powerful car. IQ is like the driver. A car without direction can either be very destructive or benign. A driver without a car is very slow in reaching his or her destination. We need both an intelligent driver (IQ) and a powerful vehicle (EQ) to reach our goals.

When persuading, we must consider the motivating force of emotions. In order to successfully persuade, we will find it necessary to touch that inherent source of drive. It is not sufficient to convince the intellect that something is right to do. We must also appeal to the heart, the emotions, that inner bastion of power within the soul. How can we do this?

If emotions are not used for manipulation but for persuasion, they can be an effective tool. A touch of emotion, a tear in the eye, is better than boo-hoo-hoo. *Tears* can be a powerful weapon. When my wife and I had one of our few differences and we were trying to persuade each other, I would sometimes use anger. She would counter with tears. Guess who won? If we deliberately conjure up tears, that's no good; but, if they come naturally, they are an excellent persuader.

I believe that the human was created by God, and in that system was placed the horsepower of emotions that enable us to survive. It is our objective to tame the wild horses, not to kill them; to use the emotions, not to eliminate them. The horsepower of our emotions is a great persuasive and motivational force that keeps us alive and drives us with great energy to fulfill our goals.

I remember being viciously cut off on the freeway one day. The event so angered me that I accelerated my car to come parallel to the offender so that I could shake my fist and yell at him. Just as I proceeded to shake my fist, I noticed that the offender was a dear friend of mine, and my fist quickly became a wave of the hand. This event let me know that under certain circumstances, it is possible to contain emotions, inhibit them, and even change them to a gesture of friendship in an instant.

Use your emotions to enhance your persuasive powers. As long as you remember to treat other people as you would be treated, persuasion can be for the good of all.

USE THE FIVE SENSES

True persuasion consists of bringing persons to the place where they want the same thing we do. Conjure up an image of your product. What does it look like? What does it sound like? What does it smell like? What does it feel like? And how does it taste? Paint a picture in the five senses. Create a desire, and soon they will be begging to get what you have for sale. In order to be an effective persuader, we let people see, hear, smell, feel, and taste our message.

My wife had secretly saved for years to take our family to Hawaii. We particularly wanted to take my mother because she was becoming depressed and needed a vacation, but Mother would not go. We argued and persuaded, but the answer was no. Then we began to appeal to the five senses. We talked about the beautiful scenery: palm trees, white sand beaches, and clear blue water. "Listen, Mother, to the crash of the surf on the sand, to the music of the ukuleles; smell the smog-free air and the exotic wild orchids; feel the warm air caressing your face and the sense of relaxation; and taste the incomparable Hawaiian food, especially at their barbecue dinners." Soon the trip became irresistible as her senses awakened to the possibilities.

REAL LIFE PERSUASION

How does a good politician persuade people to vote for him? By threats? Not in this country. All the things that go to make up a person with good people skills apply to the politician:

- He has a warm personality, offers reasonable solutions to difficult problems, shows moral integrity, keeps his word, and pays attention to his constituents' needs.

- He carefully chooses the words he uses. One bad choice and he's through.

- He knows the psychological makeup of people so that he can motivate them by making the idea he has seem to come from them.

- He uses genuine praise—no flattery.

- He is fearless in dealing with people, even a hostile crowd.

- He will confront his enemies with the truth and persuade people to vote for him by touching both their intellect and their emotions.

- He is comfortable engaging in small talk and remembers the little things like birthdays and anniversaries.

- He knows how to lead people and includes many in his campaign. Before he dares to be a leader, he submits himself in learning how to be a follower.

- He controls his anger, yet uses a measure of it to let people know he is a powerful man—serious, determined, and not to be trifled with. When Ronald Reagan was running for governor of California, he spoke to a crowd in Los Angeles. A man interrupted his speech by screaming an obscenity. Mr. Reagan, normally very friendly, rebuked the man forcefully and with anger. He let people know what he would not tolerate.

My wife and I successfully reared five children in our home. They are all wonderful people with great families. Also, at this writing, my wife and I have lived together for fifty-four years. It is our only marriage, and we have never considered a divorce. I asked my wife if this were true, and she responded with the old joke, "Divorce, no; murder, yes."

Because of the above, I dare to offer some suggestions on how to persuade family members to conform to decent behavior:

1. Start early. In dealing with children, we talked it over before we were married and set up our attitudes of behavior. Of course we changed, but we had discussed even that possibility. We planned for our children, and we planned to love them. They were no accident.

We began training methods as soon as the child was born. We decided when the child was going to eat and sleep and be loved and played with. We did not let the baby rule the roost.

2. *Stay involved.* We gave our children lots of attention. My wife didn't work or go to school; she took special care of the children, and I gave them as much time as I could.

As our children were growing up, we helped them with their school work and went to all school events. They were in sports, music, and other extracurricular activities.

3. *Include the children in decision making.* We had regular family meetings and consulted with our children concerning all decisions that affected the family.

4. *Use positive reinforcement.* We encouraged our children with compliments and rewards and seldom, if ever, engaged in corporal punishment.

We gave our children a weekly allowance, and in return we expected them to do their chores without complaint and on time.

5. *Set limits.* We gave our children as much freedom of choice as was possible, but no booze, no drugs, no smoking, no intimacy before marriage, and not too much griping or complaining.

6. *Set them free.* When our children were eighteen, we gave them freedom, but we never lost touch with them or ceased to care for them. We still give them money as they struggle with young families. A sign on the back of a recreational vehicle said, "Money isn't everything, but it sure keeps you in touch with your children."

7. *Teach them right from wrong.* We practiced and taught the highest moral values of our community. We took our children to church, and at a very early age we taught them to pray. Today, all of our children and their families go to church and serve in it.

Love, involvement, and acceptance were first, and good training was a partner.

CHECK YOUR SKILL

When we are persuading, it is logical to bargain and nego-
tiate—you do this and I'll do that. Argumentative soreheads
take the joy out of conversation as do those who try to manipulate. Learn to persuade in a friendly way.

CHAPTER 12

GIVING AND RECEIVING PRAISE

God has put something noble and good into every heart which His hand created.

—MARK TWAIN

Properly giving praise is one of the secret ingredients in people skills. People will be motivated to work harder for approval than for money. All the gold and silver in the world won't make up for disapproval and criticism, but fake praise which we call flattery meets with universal disapproval. Why do we flatter? To get something for ourselves. Why do we praise? To do something for other people. When people praise us, we need to accept it graciously as we would any gift.

RECEIVING PRAISE

I have a pet peeve: I give a compliment and the compliment is rejected. It may go something like this:
me: "I really like this cake."
she: "It's no good. I left out baking powder."
me: "It tastes very good to me."
she: "You must be having a bad day."

Another example:

me: "That's an attractive dress."

she: "This old rag? I've had it for five years, and I bought it at the Salvation Army."

me: "It looks good to me."

she: "Put on your glasses. I was going to wear it to clean the garage and then throw it away."

Here I am giving praise by passing on a sincere compliment, and I get rebuffed. I think I am being truthful and nice, and the other person takes offense. Who are these people to question my judgment and put me down?

The rule is simple: When other people give you praise, simply say, "Thank you, I'm glad you like it." Don't question their discernment.

The only exception to the above rule is when you detect that the other person is practicing deceit or pouring on the flattery to get something. Instead of giving you a fair compliment, he or she obviously is trying to set you up. When flattery is an attempt to manipulate, it comes across as a sneaky lie. What do you say to an apple polisher? Unless you like and want the flattery, tell them, "I don't think that what you are saying is true. What do you want?" Of course you can ignore the person and go your way, or you could just tell them to stop it. There is another way to say it: "I'm glad you think so highly of me; maybe someday I'll live up to it."

Sometimes high-class people of character deserve high praise and even flattery. Seldom does a superior person think that she or he is superior. Acquiring character requires humility, which doesn't allow for superiority feelings. Those who act superior are usually inferior and are trying to cover up.

I have met thousands of people in my life, and I can say that my wife is definitely a superior person. She is a woman of character, integrity, compassion, and love. She never acts superior, and my flattery of her is met with the words "that's nice" as if I were talking about someone else.

It doesn't do any good to flatter people who deserve it; they don't receive it. People who don't deserve flattery are harmed by it. So, don't flatter anyone.

GIVING PRAISE

We work for two things in this world: money (or what money represents) and approval. Christians add that we work altruistically to serve people and our God. I hate to work for ingrates, and I love appreciation. I long to hear God say, "Well done, thou good and faithful servant . . . : enter thou into the joy of thy lord" (Matt. 25:21).

I took training at the Neuro-Psychiatric Clinic at UCLA Medical Center. One day the staff assigned me a developmentally disabled twelve-year-old girl. My task was to teach her to put a square block in a square hole. She was greatly impaired. We used behavior modification techniques by rewarding her with candy every time she came close to putting a round peg in a round hole or a square peg in a square hole. After several hours, I thought I was going crazy. There was no progress whatsoever. The girl was covered with smears of chocolate. Then I stopped giving her candy and started applauding and exclaiming "good girl" whenever she came close. Soon she knew the difference between round and square. All that little girl needed was effulgent praise. Many of us are like that.

We reward people for doing the right thing or what we want done by giving them candy (money) or approval (praise). Praise works better than money.

Here are a few rules for giving praise:

BE HONEST AND SINCERE

If we are neither honest nor sincere, we will be guilty of flattery, and that's going to hurt, deceive, and disillusion. Honest praise requires careful discernment and good timing. Involve both your heart and brain when giving praise.

Some people are reluctant to receive praise; they always question the giver's sincerity. Other people are hesitant to give praise, either through fear of being considered insincere, thoughtlessness, or they are simply nonobservant. The way to not being considered insincere is to be scrupulously honest and to not give compliments for the purpose of manipulation or self-gain. The truth is not the best way; it is the *only* way. Why then do we give compliments? To encourage other people and to inspire them to do better for their own sake.

When my youngest daughter, Melody, was in the first grade, she was not doing well. I wanted to know why, so I gave her an IQ test, even though it is not definitive at that age. She scored very high—in the genius area. I asked her where she thought she was in comparison to the other kids in her class. She responded with tears, "I'm last." I then discovered that she had been put down by her classmates and maybe by the teacher (I hope not). I liberally and honestly praised her for her high IQ and told her she was in the top of the class. Almost immediately she began to do better. Now Melody has a doctorate and teaches in a prestigious university. Praise made the difference.

PRAISE EVEN SLIGHT IMPROVEMENTS

Just suppose your child, student, or friend is not a genius; in fact, she or he ranks at the bottom of the class. Your job is to move the child upward from wherever she happens to be. The slightest improvement needs your lavish praise because the only way forward is through praise, not criticism. Stupidly, I tried the critical approach on one of my children. Every time she did something wrong, I lambasted her. I did reward her with physical things, but not praise. It took her to the age of forty to recover from the critical approach—even though she was probably the brightest of all my children. To censure a child is not the method to improve him or her; *praising every improvement* is the only way.

FOCUS YOUR ATTENTION ON THE RIGHT, NOT THE WRONG

Simply stated, that's the backbone of praise—encourage the right, discourage the wrong by ignoring it (when possible).

Criticism calls attention to the wrong and by negative conditioning reinforces the predicament. All the attention some people ever get consists of someone censuring them for their bad behavior. Everyone needs attention, so they finally learn that misbehavior gives them a type of negative love (the only love they are ever going to get).

One time a convict in the prison where I worked handed me a poem he had written. I read the poem and sincerely replied, "Hey Joe, this is good; you show a lot of talent in writing." The man started to cry. I solicitously responded, "What's wrong, Joe?" He responded, "That's the first time anyone said that I ever did anything right." No wonder he was in prison. Give people the reward of praise whenever they do anything right. Don't spend too much time praising Satan by calling attention to the wrong things he has seduced people into doing.

Here is a disclaimer: I am not advocating that we ignore sin. Tough love suggests that we must deal with it. Sometimes the only thing we can do is fight sin, confront sin, and punish sin. I am advocating that we emphasize God's position more than the devil's. God is for good.

Honestly, I have noticed some zealous Christians spending more time in fighting the devil and sin than in praising the Lord. The more attention you give Beelzebub, the more he grows and the stronger he gets. Simply stated, you should pay more attention to God and count your blessings, not your curses.

DON'T OVERDO IT

Years ago E. Stanley Jones, a missionary, went around the country holding Christian retreats. At one summer camp at Big Bear in Southern California, the leader was extolling Jones's virtues before he spoke. Dr. Jones held out his hands and ducked his head as if he were being crucified on the cross. Everyone laughed, but he made his point. He was not Jesus. He was not perfect. He did not want to be worshiped. Those who desire to be worshiped are antichrists.

Sometimes we must be lavish in our praise to little children or disturbed adults, but it can backfire. I said to my little five-year-old granddaughter, "Katie, you are beautiful." She breathed a sigh of impatience and said, "I know that, Grandfather, but what difference does it make?" She didn't need much praise, just an occasional, "That's good, Katie."

One time I was trying to get a mentally deficient man out of situational depression. I praised him liberally. Finally, he declared, "I'm a genius; I'm going to be a brain surgeon." Then we couldn't get him to do anything he could do, because he was set on doing what he could not do. No matter what Jonathan Livingston Seagull or Forrest Gump have to say, we humans do have limitations. In an attempt to lift people through praise, we must not lay on them impossible burdens.

DON'T BE TOO PERSONAL
UNLESS YOU ARE VERY CLOSE

One day we went to Chinatown in Los Angeles with some very dear friends. We had to wait for a table in this high-class Chinese restaurant. The hostess was an attractive Chinese lady who wore a free-flowing black dress split from the floor to her thigh. Underneath the dress and fully exposed, she wore shimmering black stockings. My dinner friend said to her, "Those are beautiful stockings."

I thought the remark was innocuous and unnecessary, but knowing my friend, it was intended as a compliment. The hostess took offense, complained to the manager, and refused to seat us. My wife and I were very embarrassed, and I apologized for my friend, but it only made matters worse. I suppose my friend violated some cultural mores. Today, men especially must be very careful in giving attention to or praise for anything that can be taken too personally.

Every issue of our newspaper, the *Sacramento Bee*, tells of some man getting sued and losing his job for harassment. Of course some men are guilty and need to be put in their place, but I have talked to some businessmen in deep trouble who professed innocence. One man complained, "All I said to her was, 'Your fingers are graceful and pretty as you type.'" People exaggerate, but he claims she sued him for that remark.

My point is, it is all right to say, "Your work is very good"; but do not say, "Your ankles are trim and pretty." If it seems like a fine line, it is, but the line exists between appropriate and too personal.

PRAISE THE LORD

The greatest healer of human relationships; the fixer of interpersonal problems; the final solution to internecine strife; the bringer of peace, contentment, and happiness consists of changing the heart through allegiance to and worship of our God through Jesus Christ our Lord.

We need to praise God for His character which is holy and full of love, like the character of Jesus. We need to thank God for our daily bread and the blessings and luxuries He gives to us. We need to praise the Lord for our troubles, persecutions, sufferings, and even sickness. You may think I've gone too far, but no, we need to be tested and refined in the fire. We will not know happiness and joy until we experience pain and sorrow.

The Surest Way

If anyone would tell you the shortest, surest
way to happiness and all perfection, he must
tell you to make it a rule to yourself to thank
and praise God for everything that happens to
you. For it is certain that whatever seeming
calamity happens to you, if you thank and praise
God for it, you turn it into a blessing.

—William Law

CHECK YOUR SKILL

When someone offers you a compliment this week, remember to keep your response simple. "Thank you, I'm glad you like it," or "Thank you, it's nice of you to say so" are always good acknowledgments.

For extra bonus points this week, list three people you've intended to compliment but "just haven't found the right time." Make this week the right time to give them sincere praise.

CHAPTER 13

SMALL TALK AND LITTLE THINGS CAN HAVE LARGE RESULTS

Life is not made up of great sacrifices and duties, but of little things; in which smiles and kindness and small obligations, given habitually, are what win and preserve the heart and secure comfort.

—HUMPREY DAVY

Often we find ourselves in the company of a stranger. We are introduced, but we can't think of anything to say. Some people are experts at small talk, and some people are at a loss for words. What do we say when we haven't anything to say. If we remain silent, the other person is sure to eventually turn away from us and talk to someone else. Silence is not always golden. Negative people are inclined to interpret silence in a negative way.

I was invited to a banquet one time and, as luck would have it, I was seated next to a medical doctor. For whatever reasons, I kept my peace. Later in the evening, I overheard the medical doctor ask a friend of mine, "Is he retarded?" It is important to learn how to engage in polite conversation. Sometimes the choice is to keep quiet and be under suspicion, or to speak up and prove your stupidity.

Some people think carefully and then studiously weigh what they have to say, speaking with care. In my opinion they are often boring, at least tedious. A politician who doesn't want to get in hot water speaks carefully. Then again, some people talk before they think and frequently are in trouble because of off-the-wall statements. A man said to me, "I don't know what I am thinking until I hear myself say it."

Small talk needs to be more spontaneous than a serious discussion. When giving a speech or lecture, it is quite important to have notes, or at least an outline. But would you read a speech to your neighbor over a cup of coffee? No!

However, since small talk is often taken quite seriously, it requires some awareness of both the person to whom you are talking and what you are talking about. We can chitchat or even babble to close friends. Small talk around a friend can be almost anything that comes to your mind. Small talk around a stranger depends on where you are, the circumstances of the encounter, and the age and gender of the person.

SMALL TALK MADE EASY

Have you ever watched old friends get together and chatter endlessly. Small talk is a way of reducing tension, socializing, warming up a friendship, and introducing deeper topics. Of course, some conversation is just for the fun of it. We need to learn to talk and to listen when the purpose is camaraderie and friendly interchange. Listen to what the person is saying, let yourself go, and laugh heartily if appropriate. Then to show that you have listened, let it remind you of an event in your life that you can talk about just for the fun of it. Sometimes things happen to us that are extremely serious, but in the passage of time, they become very funny. I suppose that is the mind's way of reducing stress to a livable level.

What are some topics that make great icebreakers? Telling jokes, talking about your kids, your job, your personal life, your hobbies, recreation, school, political views, religion, the future, the past, the present, art, styles, the media, the weather, or the scenery. The list of small talk topics is endless.

Remember, people like to talk about themselves. Too much inconsequential small talk is boring, so allow the person to be different from you without being judgmental. In fact, it's a lot of fun to listen to a person who has concepts quite unlike ours.

Small talk is usually the introduction to important conversation, as romance is a prelude to love. I went to a wedding dinner, and the couple across from us took our name and address. She said people never meet by accident and that God had a purpose in our meeting. Look for the purpose in every casual meeting—it may be the one that will change your life.

Every summer I like to go camping with a group of good friends. We sit in a circle around a campfire, gripe a little bit about the smoke that gets in our eyes, and share events that have happened in our lives. I don't want anyone to be around that campfire who doesn't listen, and in the listening, doesn't remember that they, too, are human beings and share their experiences.

The other day a man came to visit me, and in an hour or so we solved the political problems overseas, elected a president, and reformed healthcare, education, and welfare. I enjoyed being a totalitarian dictator of the world and making right all the foolish mistakes of mankind and even womankind. What a time to show my wisdom and to listen to the profound ideas of my friend. It bothers me to have a friend come to visit, and when I ask what's going on, he or she responds, "Nothing's changed—same old thing."

I live in the woods at the foot of Mount Shasta, where few things change, and nothing really big happens (at least the news is quite mild). But I proceed to tell visitors and friends relatively insignificant events such as: The other day a mother quail pecked a blackbird who attacked one of her babies. One day a friend dropped by, and I drew such a story out for five minutes. My friend listened in awe and seemed to get permission to talk about small, trivial events in her life. Soon she was so engrossed in conversation that she revealed to me the heartrending story of her husband's suicide. Life for her had not been static or the same old thing. In order to be a true listener, you sometimes must be a stimulator of conversation.

Making good small talk does take some planning. The more you know about what's going on, the more eager you'll be to respond when someone says, "So what do you think about _____?" Keep a list of any event, no matter how trivial, that you can share with a best friend. When you start to share the trivial, you will end up revealing pockets of significance.

REMEMBER THE LITTLE THINGS

Someone said, "God is in the details." In order to be a person with people skills, we must remember the little things. Remember people's names, remember birthdays, anniversaries, and special occasions. Be polite and courteous. Be like Teddy Roosevelt and inquire about a person's loved ones, his job, school, or hobbies. This president had the reputation of knowing the names and something about the families of everyone who worked at the White House—cooks, gardeners, and chambermaids. Prove that you are interested by keeping a place in your mind (or in a notebook) filled with sufficient details to show that you are interested in someone besides yourself.

REMEMBER NAMES

One of the reasons we don't remember names is because we do not hear them. Often we are nervous when being introduced to another person, or we are concentrating on something else, and we don't actually hear the name. If you didn't hear the name, you can't remember it, so ask the person to repeat it. If he mumbles or there is too much extraneous noise, ask him to spell his name. Write it down if you have to.

Of course this method can backfire. I asked a person to spell his name and he spelled, S-M-I-T-H, and then said, "You are dumb." (I could have easily responded, "You don't know how to pronounce your own name.")

After you clearly hear a name, repeat it over and over till it fixes in your brain. When a person tells you his name, it is good to say, "I'm happy to meet you, Mr. Smith," or whatever the name is. Then use his name at every opportunity. The more you verbalize his or her name, the more likely you are to remember it.

To fix your memory on a name, pair the name with something you already know. Say to yourself, *Mr. Smith, hmmm, I went to high school with Billy Smith. I should remember that.* Or mentally compose a little doggerel or rhyme using the name, like: "Mr. Smith fell over the cliff while walking to his job at K-Mart" (or wherever he works). Believe it or not, any silly little rhyme will fix that person's name in your mind.

BE PLEASANT

It is just a little thing, but it can have tremendous results. Be pleasant, be friendly; even wild animals are calm when you are calm. Cultivate a smile. It is so elementary that we teach babies in the crib to smile. We instinctively know that they need a smiley face to get along in our world. If we scowl when we say, "I love you," people will not respond by saying, "I love you too"; rather, they will ask, "What's wrong?"

It would be a good bet that people who smile are more likely to be elected to political office. When I taught high school, I noticed how often young people were elected to class offices who had a pleasant personality and smiled a lot. Even the teachers liked them, and I have a sneaking hunch they got better grades.

How nice it is when someone hugs us and expresses interest and love.

Hugs

It's wondrous what a hug can do.
A hug can cheer you when you're blue.
A hug can say, "I love you so."
Or, "Gee, I hate to see you go."
A hug is "Welcome back again."
And "Great to see you, where've you been?"
A hug can smooth a small child's pain

And bring a rainbow after rain.
The hug: There's just no doubt about it
We scarcely could survive without it.
A hug delights and warms and charms—
It must be why God gave us arms.
Hugs are great for Fathers and Mothers,
Sweet for sisters, swell for brothers
And chances are your favorite aunts
Love them more than potted plants.
Kittens crave them, puppies love them,
Heads of State are not above them.
A hug can break the language barrier
And make your travels so much merrier.
No need to fret about your store of them.
The more you give the more there's more of 'em,
So stretch those arms without delay
And give someone a hug today!

—Dean Walley

RECOGNIZE BIRTHDAYS, ANNIVERSARIES, AND SPECIAL EVENTS

What a little thing to remember a friend's birthday with a card, flowers, or a present. If you have too many friends and you can't afford a present, how about calling them on the phone and wishing them a happy birthday, or writing a short letter saying that you are thinking of them on their day? If you are going to have friends, or even a close-knit family, you must remember the days that are special to these people.

Recently I was sick, and certain people endeared themselves to my heart with cards, letters, flowers, and visits. Little attentions are a big people skill.

SHARE THOUGHTFUL WORDS

We have talked so much about words that it seems superfluous to say, "If you want to get along with people, you must speak some nice words to them." People are so fragile. We can't stand too much criticism or negativism, and we need compliments, praise, and approval from the people we work with and live with. Even a rude-mouthed clerk in a store can ruin a day with surly talk. The custom of saying, "Have a nice day" to the people you meet leaves a good taste.

PRACTICE KIND DEEDS

My wife went shopping at Wal-Mart in Yreka, California, one day. When she came out to her car, she had a flat tire. As she was contemplating what to do, three men offered to change the tire for her. Now that makes people feel good about the human race. Be helpful and people will love you.

One day I was driving down the street in Long Beach when suddenly I saw a hub cap rolling along vigorously ahead of me. It was mine. There was so much traffic that I didn't want to stop, but I also didn't want to lose my hubcap. A young man, walking down the sidewalk, ran after my hubcap like a coyote after a rabbit. He caught it and raced alongside of my car to hand it to me. I barely had time to say thank you before he was off with a smile, a wave of his hand, and a cheery "No problem." A little thing, but I never forgot his kind help.

SHOW CONCERN FOR
PEOPLE IN TROUBLE

Visiting people in hospitals, writing to those who are bereaving or attending the funeral, expressing sympathy to those who have suffered losses, and many other demonstrations of concern can make a big difference.

One of the last messages that Jesus preached is found in the twenty-fifth chapter of Matthew. He divided people into two categories: the sheep and the goats. To the sheep he said:

Come, ye blessed of my Father, inherit the kingdom prepared for you from the foundation of the world: For I was an hungred and ye gave me meat: I was thirsty, and ye gave me drink: I was a stranger, and ye took me in; Naked, and ye clothed me: I was sick, and ye visited me: I was in prison, and ye came unto me. (Matt. 25:34–36)

He censured the goats for not doing the above and then said, "Inasmuch as ye did it not to one of the least of these, ye did it not to me" (v. 45). Jesus was saying that we must take care of people who hurt if we are to be on His side.

INCLUDE OTHERS

Few people can stand to be around a person who excludes them. Perhaps one of the greatest reasons people walk out the back door of a church is because they don't feel that they are a part. When we reject people and they don't feel included in our group, they feel like burning the house down like the girl did in the movie *Carrie*. In fact, in the past few years we have experienced a rash of disgruntled employees coming back to their places of employment and shooting their former coworkers. Nothing hurts worse than rejection. When we ostracize in a nonscriptural way, we turn others into rogues. Of course, we can't include everyone, anymore than a man or woman can marry everyone; but excluding someone from our circle must be done with delicacy, compassion, and sensitivity to the feelings of others. Everyone is entitled to his or her place and the feeling of security in that place.

There are a number of things we can do to include people:

1. At church, walk around and shake hands. Greet people by name and introduce yourself to visitors. People sometimes complain that a church is cold. Don't let that be said of your church.

2. Be friendly at your workplace. Greet new employees and remember to say hello wherever you meet them.

3. At family gatherings our relatives can be quite sensitive. Be sure you circulate and make everyone feel a part of the family.

4. Give a greeting to those people who ignore you. Let the charge of "unfriendly" be on them, not you.

Cities of America are being overwhelmed by the rising violence in youth gangs. In September 1995, a Los Angeles family drove down a dead-end street seeking a shortcut home. A belligerent young gang defending its territory opened fire and killed a three-year-old child. Events like this occur daily. Why? No easy answer springs to the forefront; but a significant contributing factor is the breakdown of the family which leaves young people with no place for acceptance outside the gangs.

Notes like the following are not at all unusual in today's climate and show the results of rejection:

> Blackville, S.C.—A student suspended for violence, whose father said was picked on because he was small, walked into the high school Thursday, shot and seriously wounded a teacher, then killed himself. . . . Other high school students would lock the boy, who was less than 5 feet tall, in lockers or dump him upside-down in trash cans.
>
> —Associated Press

Some years ago, the African-American people were excluded from equal treatment in our society. Jackie Robinson, a great baseball player, was the first black allowed to play professionlly. That was in the years 1947 to 1956 when the Big Leagues opened up to blacks. When I was a young man, blacks could not vote, had to ride on the back of a bus, couldn't drink from the same water fountain or go to the same restroom as whites, had to step aside for whites on a public sidewalk, and myriad other restrictions.

I know a little of how they feel. I have been in a wheelchair most of my life and have experienced much exclusion. In 1970, I went to UCLA to take some classes in special education to learn better how to deal with physical and mental handicaps. The special education building had no access for wheelchairs, steep stairs to get in, and restrooms that couldn't be occupied by a wheelchair. I had to crawl up the stairs, dragging my wheelchair behind me. Thank God, it has improved. But, I know what exclusion does to the psyche and interpersonal relationships.

Little things are sometimes the crucial life-and-death difference. From memory I would like to quote:

The Horseshoe Nail

For want of a nail, the shoe was lost;
For want of a shoe, the horse was lost;
For want of a horse, the rider was lost;
For want of a rider, the message was lost;
For want of a message, the battle was lost;
For want of a battle, the kingdom was lost;
All for the want of a horseshoe nail.

CHECK YOUR SKILL

Little things do make a difference. Just a little conversation can often save a life. Just a little attention to detail can bring happiness, peace, and contentment to those who need us. Make an effort to take a little time to pay heed to those who are excluded, and soon we will have a happy family.

The World's Greatest Need

A little more kindness and a little less greed;
A little more giving and a little less need;
A little more smile and a little less frown;
A little less kicking a man when he's down;
A little more "we" and a little less "I";
A little more laughs and a little less cry;
A little more flowers on the pathway of life;
And fewer on graves at the end of the strife.

—Source Unknown

PART III

FINAL THOUGHTS ON PEOPLE SKILLS

CHAPTER 14

HOW TO
MAKE ENEMIES

Being miserable and treating other people like dirt is every New Yorkers right.

— MAYOR OF NEW YORK

Why do I include a chapter in a book on people skills on making enemies? Because without the negative *no*, the positive *yes* is meaningless. "No, no, no," the young woman said to other suitors. Because of her no to them, her yes to me made me jump for joy, and I married her. Now, if my wife doesn't say no to other men, her yes to me is worthless. Our generation has forgotten that the positive pole of the battery does not work without being grounded in the negative.

Just suppose we got very positive and took the negative "Thou shalt *nots*" out of the Ten Commandments. They would then say, "Thou *shalt* commit adultery," "Thou *shalt* kill," "Thou *shalt* steal," etc. *Yes* is one of God's most important words, but before *yes* is operative, *no* is an imperative. When we learn the nos, we know much better the yeses.

We know how to appreciate health when we have experienced sickness. Happiness would be an unknown condition if it had never been contrasted with sadness. Goodness takes its sparkle from the ugliness of sin. When we have thoroughly learned what not to do, we then know what to do. When lots of trouble comes your way, consider that gold is impure unless refined by fire.

The Bible says, "For whom the LORD loves He chastens, And scourges every son whom He receives" (Heb.12:6, NKJV). Why? Because love cannot be experienced without the pain of correction. We must take the no of God in order to receive His eternal yes. We are to make this sinful world as happy as we can through positive closeness to our God. We choose to go the positive way, not because we ignore the negative, but because we know full well what it is. We are in this world to be tried by the negative in order to learn how to appreciate the high values of the positive.

A good way to develop positive people skills to win others for us is to learn some clear-cut negative ways to make enemies and set people against us:

1. *Tell people the blunt truth as you see it—no quarter given.* You have heard people say, "Call a spade a spade." What they really mean is, "I have found a way to dig your grave with my harsh words." When people say, "This is for your own good," they mean, "I have found a way to hurt you," and they do.

Don't speak the truth in love. The truth is a weapon; beat people to death with it.

2. *Be rude, discourteous, and frank.* Certain words may be brutally true, and also inflammatory—use them. Don't soften your speech to adhere to the customs of the people around you. No euphemisms for you.

Before the Gulf War, Saddam Hussein, leader of Iraq, was very appalled because we did not show him respect. One of the major but hidden reasons for the war was Saddam's need to be treated like royalty. Thousands of his people died because he thought we were rude and discourteous when we called him names.

Call people names. Maybe you can start a war.

3. Swear, curse, and use vulgar language. Talk in obscenities. Show people how tough and hip you are. You can be assured that even convicts will avoid you. Crude language turns off both the good and the bad. The most beautiful and effective speech can be nullified by a single alley word. We can effectively drive away the most loyal follower with a curse. A curse a day will keep them away.

4. Argue with everything that people say. Build yourself up by putting others down. Who cares about their self-esteem. Right or wrong, win the great debate of life by disagreeing with other people's opinions and "see how they run." Even if they win an argument, don't admit it. Heaven forbid, you wouldn't want to win a friend, would you?

5. Defend yourself against any suggestion. Take every suggestion as a personal insult and vigorously defend your position without listening to a word other people say. Lo and behold, other people will stop talking to you. Think that every word people utter has a secret meaning against you. Take umbrage, develop paranoia, fight back—even before they attack—and watch them fade away.

6. Let everyone know that you know it all. After all, you are an expert in every field. At least you can be down on what you are not up on. Bluff your way through; who will know the difference? Forget the saying that even a little child can sometimes lead us. Adopt the superior know-it-all attitude that builds instant resistance from the people around you. Even if others are right, make them look wrong.

7. Talk loudly at every occasion. You, of course, want to be the star and monopolize every conversation and situation, so talk loudly to keep anyone from interrupting or taking the center stage away from you. Soon you will be screaming to an empty room.

8. Interrupt every conversation with your own opinions. Don't listen. What do they know! Make them listen to you. Your experience, your knowledge, and your wisdom is all that counts. Put people down, and discount everything they say.

Soon you will be talking to yourself. What a glorious experience that will be.

9. Make no effort to say any good thing about anyone, except yourself. When people tell you about their achievements, say, "That's no achievement." Then remind them of all of the great things you have done, intend to do, or could do if you wanted. Even if a person has graduated or written a successful book or gotten a promotion, never say, "Congratulations" or "How wonderful." Make it a point to discount their achievements and remind them that they're not so hot. The response "I could have done better" will win you lasting enmity.

10. Search for every inconsistency that you can find in other people and make it look as bad as you can. Never look for the good, always exacerbate the bad. If you try hard enough you can even make God look like a devil. A favorite saying could be: "People are no good." Trust no one, suspect everyone, and everyone will suspect you. It will be great fun to live in a world of criminals.

11. Gossip about other people. It will make your best friends believe you are gossiping about them behind their backs. Oh, what a happy life! People will wince when they see you coming.

12. Invent stories, lie, and slander people. If negative gossip doesn't get you properly rejected, try making up vicious lies. Who can defend themselves against certain false accusations? What an effective way to disrupt people, families, and organizations. If you are clever enough, you can even get the preacher fired.

13. Talk about yourself at every opportunity and don't let other people talk about themselves. You must be the center of every conversation and situation. Don't let other people get any credit—after all, life swirls around you. Boost yourself and no one else, and soon you will be a one-man booster band with no one listening to your music but you.

14. Desperately try to please everyone. Put yourself down and fawn over others. It can be a subtle way of calling attention to yourself. Let people use you and then abandon you. They will consider you to be a wimp and walk all over you with great disrespect. You know how much fun it is to use people and then despise them—sadistic pleasure. Even more fun is to let yourself be taken advantage of and then forsaken—masochistic pleasure.

15. *Let your value system change with everyone who has a different moral code.* Don't stand for anything, and everyone will knock you down. Do what the undisciplined crowd wants, and you will be the first one to go to jail. Listen, learn, and follow the convicts. When you get out of prison, don't worry; you will soon be back. As an added benefit, you will break the hearts of everyone who loves you.

16. *Follow your feelings.* Don't use your mind; use your emotions. Get emotional, no matter how unreasonable. You know that the head bone needs to be connected to the heart bone to put love and affection in life. But to disenchant people, put the heart bone in place of the head bone. When your feelings rule without reason, people will think you are crazy—and you will be.

17. *Be tough and demanding.* Don't give anyone the benefit of the doubt. Be quite loose in your demands on yourself but be perfectionistic with other people. Don't give compliments, rule with rebukes, and call attention to deficiencies. Shape people up—who cares whether they like you or not. Give yourself the benefit of every doubt and don't give anyone else any latitude at all.

18. *Get deeply involved in the "ain't it awfuls."* All news can be changed into bad news. Search the news media diligently for all stories about crime and violence. Cluck your tongue and tell these stories with embellishments. Emphasize your bad views to such an extent that people will think there is no good news.

19. *Expect the worst in people—and you'll get it.* Don't give people a good reputation to live up to; rather, predict that they will do the wrong thing. You won't be disappointed. If you try hard enough you may be able to turn good people into bad ones with your evil expectations.

20. *Demand justice for yourself, but never give it to others.* Demand that everything and everyone turn out just like you think it should. The Bible says in Amos 5 that we should concentrate on doing justice, not seeking it. Ignore the Bible. Raise holy heck, sue them, shape them up. Work so hard in forcing people to do what you think is right that they won't see how unjust you have become.

21. *Be deeply prejudiced against certain races, cultures, other denominations, and various ways of looking at life.* Make your favorite saying, "The only good [name a race] is a dead one." If they are not of your race, culture, or religion, search history for every evil thing they have done and bring it up at every occasion. Be a bigot and be proud of it. Perhaps you can start a riot.

22. *Hate everyone who doesn't agree with you.* Agree with people to their faces but ridicule and belittle them behind their backs. What right does anyone have to form a different opinion than yours. Take it personally and fight everything you don't like. Get them for disagreeing and soon you will be got.

23. *By all means use God and religion to your own advantage.* Don't worship Him or accept Him; rather ask: "If God were a God of love, why do little children suffer?" And, of course, don't search for an answer, but use the question to justify your own meanness.

Pretend you are very pious and religious—it's good for business. Become an elder or deacon in the church, and use status to take advantage of people. Use God, use the faith, but don't let Christianity change your heart, or you might have to change your ways.

24. *Criticize strongly every charitable program, every church, every social and political action group.* You will have an excuse for not being involved in any good thing. It is particularly effective to pass on gossip or invent stories about group leaders. You can put down the whole group if you can find one bad apple.

25. *Don't bother to remember names, birthdays, anniversaries, or any other special occasions.* You will come across as a thoughtless

bore, and people will gladly avoid you. To make it even more effective, pout and be insulted if people fail to remember your name. Especially put up a big fuss if your wife or children don't remember your birthday, but by all means conveniently forget theirs.

26. Never write, and seldom visit, friends and family. What an excellent way to eliminate them from your life. Add insult to injury by becoming hostile and offended when family members and friends don't write or visit you.

27. Treat your parents with great disrespect. It will guarantee that your children will treat you with disrespect as you grow older. Add the little touch of whining and complaining about everything parents or children do for you.

28. No matter how generous people are, find something wrong. If a person gives you a gift, never say, "Thank you" or "Oh, how nice"; rather, say, "It isn't the right size" or "I hate that color" or "Can I exchange this for something I want?" Even if people get together and buy you a new car, take it back to the dealer and get the one you really want—or try to get the cash instead. If your children send you on a trip, constantly harp about what you didn't like about it. The above techniques will keep people from being charitable with you.

29. Use threats to get what you want. Intimidate and beat the other person down to get what you want. If you can get away with it, use physical force—or at least threaten violence—to bring people around. Rule by out-raging and out-shouting; with thundering, fulminating warnings, get your own way. Soon you will be on the way alone.

30. Flatter people. Try to manipulate people with a smooth line and sweet words. Don't mean a word you say, though. It doesn't have to be true, just butter them up and then use them. Develop a clever line, and you can get your way. Woe betide you if they find out.

31. Use sarcasm and sneer a lot. Never be guilty of talking straight: use snide remarks, innuendoes, and subtle implications. Make people feel put-down and keep them that way with scorn and skepticism. Oh, how big it will make you look (in you own eyes) when you can make them look little. You wouldn't want anyone to like you, would you?

Notice the sarcasm. If you didn't like it, you got the message. If you did like it, you are in trouble.

CHECK YOUR SKILL

Review the ways to make enemies. Select three that you're particularly adept at and practice *not* doing them for at least a week.

CHAPTER 15

OVERCOMING FEAR OF PEOPLE

People are lonely because they build walls instead of bridges.

—Joseph Fort Newton

Fear of people often results in painful encounters or sometimes hermitlike behavior. We need to conquer fear, particularly fear of people. If we had no fear, we would be reckless with our lives in a dangerous world. However, when we have too much fear, we paralyze our lives with worry, anxiety, phobias, and withdrawal from contact with people. Natural or normal fear is part of the human gift to preserve and protect our lives. But when the natural attaches itself to cruel events that we acquire from experience, it can terrorize us with false fears and can render us mentally ill if carried to its final conclusion. The death of the fear of people often requires a complicated desensitization process.

WHAT FEAR DOES TO YOU

Fear inhibits the effects of the healing power of good relationships because fear is the opposite of faith. People consumed by fear have weakened the power of their faith in themselves, in each other, and in God; this enables the devil to appear strong.

Fear weakens relationships and stifles love. When fear comes in, faith goes out, or is paralyzed. A person with terrorizing fear runs when no man pursues.

However, a little fear is not always bad. When fear is nonexistent, life can be boring, inefficient, and unsatisfying. A moderate amount of fear and anxiety (not too little, not too much) motivates us and adds zest to life. In addition, a little fear keeps us from harm's way.

But when fear is great, we begin to experience crippling physical, psychological, defensive, and spiritual reactions. Any people skills we have lose all effectiveness. We are too frightened of people to be able to use our techniques.

Excessive fear can produce ulcers, headaches, skin rashes, backaches, and a variety of other physical problems. Almost everyone has experienced stomach discomfort ("butterflies"), shortness of breath, an inability to sleep, increased fatigue, loss of appetite, and a frequent desire to urinate during times of anxiety and fear. Less conscious are changes in blood pressure, muscle tension, digestive processes, and chemical changes in the blood. If these are temporary, they cause little, if any, harm. When they persist over time, though, the body begins to break under the pressure.

Excessive fear can cause the body to mimic physical illness so accurately that the best of medical diagnosticians can be fooled. A high degree of fear and worry can cause a stomach ulcer that will perforate the stomach lining just as efficiently as toxic food will. Fear can fire a discharge of hormones that will create a noxious acid condition from inside the body which is as deadly as poisons swallowed from outside the body.

Research has shown that fear and anxiety reduce one's level of productivity, shorten one's attention span, hinder performance skills, interfere with problem solving, block effective communication, arouse panic, cause undesirable physical symptoms such as paralysis or intense headaches, stifle creativity and originality, hinder the capacity to relate to others smoothly, dull the personality, and interfere with the ability to think or to remember. Unhealed psychological problems can be the origin of psychosomatic illnesses which are just as debilitating as physical illness.

Even Christians when fraught with worry and distracted by pressures, find that there is a lack of time for prayer, decreased ability to concentrate on Bible reading, reduced interest in worship, impatience, and sometimes bitterness. Our Christian skill in dealing with people is lost through our fear of them.

SOURCES OF FEAR

Where does all this fear come from? Fear of people is encouraged by the reports of war and violence all over the world. I used to pick up hitchhikers and met some valuable people. Now, with the high incidence of crime, I am afraid to pick up anyone. A subtle but powerful force is at work. A large portion of it comes through television. It can be easily illustrated through the influence of a book of twenty years ago titled *The Exorcist* by William Peter Blatty, which was turned into a terrifying film seen by millions of people. The film vividly and graphically depicts the tremendous power of Satan, a power which, when matched up with the mechanism of fear, seems even greater than the power of Jesus.

With all of Hollywood's special-effects comes a spine-tingling display of Satan's work through a little girl, Regan, whom Satan turns into a hideous monster that attacks two priests in a physical, spiritual, and psychological way.

Since that movie was produced, it has received widespread viewing; plus, it has spawned scores of follow-up films which have been seen by millions of people, young and old. Movies and books with the theme of powerful, fearful demons and devils overcoming the representatives of the Christian faith from all persuasions are too numerous to list. Such films as all three *Omen* movies, *Friday the 13th*, and countless others leave the overall impression that Satan, his kingdom, and his powers are strong while the Christians empowered by the Holy Spirit are weak.

The theme of weak, wimpy Christians and strong satanic influences conditions the minds of people to believe that the fearful horror and gross images of satanic evil are stronger than the love and power of Jesus Christ. If the devil can make every bush look like a bear, he can keep Christians in their cabin. His lying message of fear becomes real, and it destroys our ability to care for people. This conditioning along with severe crime, violence, and excessive stress creates an atmosphere of fear and suspicion among all people.

OVERCOMING FEAR

What are some of the things we can do to overcome our fear of life and people so that we can use people skills to make our way more pleasant?

EXAMINE YOURSELF

We need to examine fear as a powerful, destructive lifeforce. First Corinthians 11:28 states, "But let a man examine himself." We must ask ourselves some searching questions concerning our weakness and our strength. Basically, we need to ask ourselves why we are afraid of people, and just what resources we have to conquer the fear. It very well may be that our fear is not as fierce as we believe, and our strengths may be greater than we realize.

We begin by identifying our strengths. Often when they are hidden in the inner recesses of our minds, we can easily be like the servant who hid his talent in the ground. God wants us to recognize our talents and use them. Often the only thing we need to do to conquer our fears, worries, anxieties, and doubts is to utilize the strength that almighty God has already given us.

The first step in doing away with fear is to take an honest inventory in which we examine our past, our present, and our future.

FACE YOUR FEARS

After identification, we must face our fears. Fear that is not faced goes underground, becomes secret, and develops into an unconscious problem that can be very fierce indeed. Hidden fear shows itself in strange, bizarre, and harmful conduct. We must face our fears or face the consequence of a cowardly, fearful personality.

Fear has a way of hiding. Some people are filled with fear, but can't identify the fears. Fear specializes in the darkness of night, in damp corners, in ignorance, and in the unknown. Sometimes all we have to do to conquer fear is to walk up and eyeball it. "Who are you, sir? What is your name? Where do you live? Where do you come from? Why are you living in my house? What purpose do you have for existence?" If we name our fears, often they will disappear.

When an angry grizzly bear charges in our direction, only a lump of clay (or anything without intelligence or feeling) would fail to have fear. We know what genuine, constructive fear is. It keeps us alive and protects us from harm. When we know exactly what we are afraid of, fear can be a friend; but when we are saturated with fear, and there is no grizzly or anything else in sight, we are in trouble.

Remember when Joshua sent twelve spies into the promised land? Ten of the spies saw the people of the land as giants and themselves as grasshoppers. They were filled with fear. The other two spies also saw the giants as something to fear, but their power under the leadership of God was greater than fear. Not only must we face up to our fears, we must recognize and claim our strengths, our powers, our relationship with God, and His ability to help us conquer any threatening giants.

ASK FOR HELP

It very well may seem that asking for help is a trite truism. Of course, when a person is afraid, he or she will obviously ask for help. Unfortunately, not always! Instead of calling out for help, our voice pours out screams of terror—often missing the help that is right by our side.

Every parent remembers calming a child who has had a nightmare. Remember how you held the child and comforted and soothed away his or her fears. Our little three-year-old boy awoke one night screaming in terror. We dashed into his room and turned on the light. As we tried to calm him down, he grabbed his teddy bear and flung it from the bed. "My teddy bear wet the bed and then bit me," he sobbed. Never again would he sleep with the teddy bear.

We are all children sometimes. We all need some parenting. If you are afraid, take solace from your friends or relatives. Let them hold you and comfort you and soothe you. It is a terrible thing to be all alone, to scream in anguish, and face our nightmares without any help. Ask almost anyone around you, and you will find a mothering and fathering instinct to comfort you.

When you are overcome with fear, like Simon Peter sinking in the tempestuous sea, cry out for help. Your fear of people will drown your ability to relate to people. One way out is to ask for help. Jesus, who walks on water, will rescue you. Don't let your fears sink you; let Him pull you up so you can, once again, walk on water with the Master.

Get Involved with Something besides Fear

Luke 5:10 says, "Do not be afraid, from now on you will catch men" (NIV). When we find ourselves afraid, we need to immediately turn our attention to our purpose, to our goals, or to our work. Do not dwell on the fear. Get involved with your job, a part of which is to catch men (or deal with people).

Fear is a psychological disease of inactivity. A hard-working person seldom has time to succumb to fear. When fear comes, don't just stand there and let it consume you. Get up, and go to work doing what God has assigned to you to fulfill your existence on this earth. Following are some simple, yet constructive steps you can take:

Start where you are. Make your bed, clean up the room (even if you just pick up one piece of paper), shave, bathe, brush your teeth, and do whatever needs to be done in the immediate vicinity of you.

Work on your procrastinations. Write that letter home, fix that broken window, and try to unburden yourself from the things you have intended to do.

Start a schedule. Some things need to be put on a regular schedule that is seldom broken: get up at a prescribed time, go to bed on time (no dawdling), and exercise regularly. When you schedule your life, it leaves less time to be absorbed by fear.

Keep a journal of the good things that have happened to you. When our mind is full of the fear of people, we have exaggerated the worst. Compensate by writing down the best.

Deliberately force yourself to be friendly with people. You will be surprised at their warm responses.

KEEP ON KEEPING ON

Everyone has some problems with the fear of people. Do not let a few ugly experiences stop you. No one can live this life without fear, anxiety, worry, doubts, insecurity, inferiority, and lack of self-esteem. Conquering our problems is a lifelong task. Don't be discouraged. Keep on fighting.

The apostle Paul said in Philippians 3:13–14 that he had not already arrived, but that he was going to forget those things which were behind and press on toward the high calling of God in Christ Jesus. He was not going to give up but would keep on keeping on. Enduring to the end is one of the ways to conquer fear. Life consists of one thing after another. Just when we think we have our problems licked, another set comes our way. We must resolve to fight to the end. When the Great Coach in the sky taps us on the shoulder and says, "Your game is over," then we can throw down the ball and walk off the field. Until that time, no matter how tired or exhausted you might feel, pick up the ball and keep on playing.

DEVELOP A STRONG FAITH

Faith is the opposite of fear, so faith is the final answer. The more you develop your faith, the fewer will be your fears of people. Even great men and women of God have had moments of terrorizing fear and sometimes long periods of sustained phobias. Most people vacillate. Sometimes they have great faith and little fear; sometimes the faith gets a little weak, and the fear grows strong. When these times of fear come upon us, the question is: "How do we increase our faith?" We will find the answer in the following ways:

Faith is contagious. We catch it. Faith comes from association with people of faith. Little children who are afraid catch their fears, not so much from events, but from parents. Mothers who are terrorized by things that go bump in the night raise children who have the same fear. We catch the emotion of fear when we spend time around people who have fear. We catch bravery from people who are brave, unless they spend time making fun of our fears. When a person is criticized or condemned or put to shame because of his or her fear, it does not cure it, but makes it sink deep into the system. Here is a truism: you can't scare fear out of people—just as you can't condemn it out.

Faith comes from "good things." Increase your faith by reading uplifting literature and turning the television off. When TV is bombarding your mind with occult, devilish, terrorizing, frightening events, turn it off. Do not let your mind be saturated by serial killer stories from the newspaper, radio, or TV. Do not spend your precious time on earth telling ghost stories, even with a friend. Anyone whose mind is filled with fear risks driving out faith.

Good reading, good music, good art—in fact, good anything—is appropriate because it is uplifting. It makes us happy, not sad. It brings peace, not upset. If you want to take fear out of your life, let your life be saturated by beautiful, inspirational thoughts.

Righteousness brings about a stronger faith. We increase our faith by prayer, meditation, and deliberate concentration on the powerful, beautiful, and wholesome things of God. The problem with sermons that threaten hellfire and damnation is that they do the opposite of what they intend to do. These sermons try to make people fear sin and evil people and turn to God. Instead, they often make people afraid of God and then they turn to sin and think all people are evil.

Not so long ago there was a television program entitled *Scared Straight*. Some convicts tried to scare some delinquent young people into being good. At first everyone raved about how effective this wonderful program was. Yet after a few years it was discovered that those delinquent youth had become more criminal, not less. You can't scare people into righteousness or faith.

Faith develops through our testimony. Faith does not grow in a dark closet anymore than a sunflower does. Faith requires an expression. It grows when we pass it on. Faith kept to ourselves diminishes even to the point of disappearance, and fear fills the gap.

The important things that children need to acquire from their parents are the feelings of acceptance, self-esteem, and self-confidence. Without these "I believe in you child; now you can believe in yourself" feelings, a child cannot grow properly, and he will certainly have feelings of fear or suffer from mental illness. Most parents instinctively know that you can neglect food, water, and shelter with less damage than when you neglect to give the child faith—faith in you the parent, faith in himself or herself, faith in people, faith in life, and faith in God. If the child believes, the child can face the adversities of life fearlessly.

Do people a favor. Let them know that you believe in them. It will give them a reason to live. Let them know that you believe in yourself, and they'll want to be around you. Let them know that you believe in life, and it will help to take away their fear of it. Let them know that you believe in God, and it will help them to have faith.

Demonstration builds faith. When people see you run with no one pursuing, they have an idea that there might be some secret demon, so they run too. When you scream out in fear, it makes people afraid. When you allow your eyes to widen with fear and your knees to tremble, people turn their gaze from you to protect themselves from the contagious disease you have.

An old story tells of General Tulare, just before the battle of Tours, shaving in his tent. An aide heard him exclaim when he cut himself, "Tremblest thou vile carcass? Thou wouldst tremble even more if thou knewest where I was going to take thee today." The general had strong control over his body's natural tendency to be afraid of death. If the general demonstrated fear in front of his troops, for sure, the battle would be lost. If we demonstrate fear, even in front of ourselves, it exacerbates the fear and leaves us running for our life.

True faith can stand the test of doubt. Allow your faith to be questioned without getting angry or fearful or skeptical. The Bible says it is impossible to please God without faith (see Heb. 11:6). It does not say it is impossible to be well-pleasing to God without facts. Facts are scientific and provable. Faith must have enough facts to make it reasonable, but does not demand enough facts to make it an absolute. Faith is believing in the highest, holiest, and best, sometimes in the face of the lowest, most ugly, and terrible things. Faith can grow on the battlefield where it looks like there is no God. Do not allow someone's challenge to your faith to upset you. Think about it. Maybe God is trying to lift you up a step higher. Sometimes the only way our faith can grow is when it is challenged.

Faith is ever growing toward Christlikeness. Develop a strong conscience and wisdom from awareness of the truth of God. We need to study to show ourselves approved unto God (2 Tim. 2:15). People who are poor Bible students and have not studied or read enough or associated with people of powerful faith sometimes have a faith so full of errors that it is ineffective. We need a true faith, an intelligent faith, a loving faith, a practical faith, and a faith that works because it is founded on the One who says, "I am the way, the truth, and the life" (John 14:6). Such a faith does not come cheaply. Many people who are "babes in Christ" remain that way. Baby faith does not produce men and women of God who have power. Baby faith requires constant support. As Christians we are to never cease growing, learning, and acquiring a mature Christlike faith. As we grow in faith, we will shrink in fear of life and people.

USE PRACTICAL WISDOM

You cannot conquer fear with fear. Many of us seem to believe that people would behave in more socially acceptable ways if someone in authority just threatened them enough. In recent years, for instance, nationwide campaigns against sexually transmitted diseases, the use of hard drugs, cigarette smoking, and the dangers of not wearing seat belts have employed the scare-'em-to-death approach—that is, the main thrust of the propaganda has been to describe in exquisite detail the terrible consequences of various types of misbehavior.

But are such threats really as effective as we sometimes think them to be? The experimental evidence suggests that the actual effects of the punitive approach are more subtle and complex than we might previously have guessed. Irving Janis and Seymour Feshbach investigated the effects of fear-arousing communications on high school students and reported it in the *Journal of Abnormal and Social Psychology* in 1983. These scientists picked as their topic, dental hygiene, or the dangers of not taking care of your teeth. They wrote three different fifteen-minute lectures on tooth decay. The first was a "high fear" lecture that contained seventy-one references to pain, cancer, paralysis, blindness, mouth infections, inflamed gums, ugly or discolored teeth, and dental drills. The second, or "moderate fear," lecture was somewhat less threatening; but the third, or "minimal fear," lecture was quite different. It made no mention at all of pain and disease, but rather suggested ways of avoiding cavities and decayed teeth through proper dental hygiene.

Janis and Feshbach presented each of the three appeals to a different group of fifty high school students (a fourth group of students heard no lecture at all and thus served as a control group). Janis and Feshbach found that immediately afterward, the subjects exposed to the high-fear lecture were highly impressed with what they heard. The students also admitted that the lecture got them very worried about the health of their own teeth. A week later, however, only 28 percent of them had brushed their teeth more often, and 20 percent of them were actually doing worse.

In marked contrast, the low-fear students were not particularly impressed with the lecture, but a week later 50 percent of them were "brushing better" and only 14 percent were doing a worse job.

The high fear appeal apparently evoked strong emotional responses in the students, many of whom thought that being frightened was somehow "good for them." As one student said, "Some of the pictures of decayed teeth went to extremes, but they probably had an effect on most of the people who wouldn't want their teeth to look like that. I think it is good because it scares people when they see the awful things that can happen."

Despite this student's beliefs, when it came to actually changing behaviors, the high-fear message simply didn't work as well as did the low-fear message. In fact, the high-fear propaganda seemed to have produced exactly the opposite long-term effect than one might have predicted.

There seems to be a tendency for people to repress or deliberately forget frightening information. Your emotions can arouse you, but they don't always direct you in your thoughts and behavior. Fear-inducing communications focus your attention on problems and not on solutions.

Use logical thinking to dispel fear. To renew your mind you must straighten out your thinking. Most people in the kingdom of fear are thinking in a hopeless circle. Perhaps fear begins with a feeling of rejection. Out of rejection grows a feeling of insecurity, not knowing whom to trust. Insecurity is another manifestation of fear, and out of it grows a feeling of guilt. Out of guilt grows a need to be punished. If no one else will punish us, we volunteer to punish ourselves. How do we do that? We make ourselves miserable and unacceptable; hence, we have a vicious circle that can only be straightened out by logical thinking.

Thinking logically involves the law of cause and effect. When we look at our lawn and see that it is dried up, the law of cause and effect will tell us that it needs water or some type of fertilizer. Illogical thinking, on the other hand, states that the lawn dried up because the stars have ordained it; this logic leads to a powerful misunderstanding of life which leads to fear.

Use the techniques of counterconditioning. Fear often comes from conditioning. That is, natural fear is connected to an unnatural item. The natural fear of loud noises becomes connected to the fear of the toy the child is playing with when the loud noise occurs. Fear has been conditioned. God gave us a few fears to protect us from harm. Under the adversities of life, we have transferred normal fear to abnormal fear. A simple answer is to transfer back.

S. H. Kaines in his book *Mental Depressions and Their Treatment* reported a young medical student (J. M.) who feared the sight of blood. This young man considered giving up the study of medicine because each time he walked into an operating room, he keeled over in a dead faint.

Kaines first attempted to determine the causes for this response and tried to change the boy's attitude toward medicine—but he also tried a step-by-step deconditioning treatment. J. M. was told to walk into the operating room during an operation and then immediately to walk out. On the second day J. M. went into the room, counted to five, and then walked out. On the third day J. M. was told to stay a full minute before leaving. On subsequent days, J. M. stayed longer and longer.

Two weeks later, when J. M. was supposed to stay ten minutes, he got so interested in the operation that he stayed on until it was completed. Thereafter, Kaines reports, J. M. had no trouble at all—even when called on to assist in operations. His "blood phobia" appeared to be gone for good.

There is an old and ancient saying used in modern times by the Dale Carnegie course: "Do the thing you fear, and the death of fear is certain." This method is called in psychology counterconditioning.

In one of psychology's most famous experiments, John B. Watson and his wife, Rosalie, taught a child named Albert to become afraid of a gentle and placid white rat. At the beginning of the study, Albert was unafraid of the animal and played with it freely. While Albert was doing so one day, the Watsons deliberately frightened the boy by sounding a terrifying noise behind him. Albert was unpleasantly startled and began to cry. Thereafter, he avoided the rat and cried if it was brought close to him. Once this bond was fixed, the fear response could also be elicited by showing Albert any furry object.

Later Albert was changed back to his innocent state through positive reconditioning. The Watsons simply praised Albert by saying, "good boy" as they gradually presented the rat from a distance to close at hand. In other words, they praised every improvement, no matter how slight, until the fear was removed.

Harry Brink was a big, strong carpenter who set records in his speed of hanging doors. He could lift a heavy door with one hand as he used tools in the other hand to plane the door. People came from miles around to watch this affable giant do the work of six men in a single day. But Harry Brink was afraid of people, particularly of speaking in public. One day he tried to give a short speech, and he fainted on the platform. He asked me to help him. I took him to a speech class that I taught and let him watch other people speak. Gradually, I brought him closer to the front until the great day in which he stood up and said, "Hello, my name is Harry Brink." From that simple beginning, Harry now lectures to churches and universities.

To conquer any specific fear, it is necessary to face the fear, gradually connecting it with something pleasant until the fear disappears. A lady who was afraid of heights had transferred her fear to elevators, ladders, escalators, and anything that went up. The fear had become so bad that she was unable to walk up the steps into her own home. The more she thought about the fear, the worse it got. It always does. The lady was started on a program of eating her favorite food as she watched some pictures of people climbing stairs. Gradually various rewards were given to her as she approached walking up the stairs. She soon learned to step up one step, and her journey toward conquering the fear had begun.

Any fear can gradually be eliminated by slowly allowing it to be saturated with good.

Use relaxation techniques to cure fear. When a person is afraid, he or she becomes very tense and stressed. The opposite of tension and stress is relaxation. Jesus knew this when He came to the disciples who were locked in a room for fear of the Jews. He said, "Peace be unto you" (Luke 24:36). He could have just as easily told them to relax and be tranquil.

A major part of relaxation therapy consists of teaching the patient to relax voluntarily by alternately tensing and then relaxing muscles. You can't very well be tense or anxious at the same time that you are physically limp as a wet rag.

You can acquire the ability to relax at your own verbal or mental command. Once you have mastered this skill, you can order the muscles in your body to relax even when you are faced with fear. If you happen to suffer from a phobia, one of the best ways of dealing with it is to learn how to relax.

Use role playing or "acting as if . . ." If a person acts brave, it is inclined to make him or her feel brave. Use your imagination to pretend that you have a certain emotion, and that act will create the emotion. Just suppose you see a bear. The sight of that bear is likely to invoke the feeling of fear. Cannon-Bard said, "We see something to fear, and then we feel the fear." William James said, "We feel fear, and then identify what we see as something to fear." One is saying that events cause feelings of fear; the other is saying the feeling of fear structures events. In other words, don't let the event inspire fear. Act as if you are not afraid, and you won't be afraid. Do not let an event cause an emotion. You control the emotion by acting as if it did not exist.

CHECK YOUR SKILL

The Christian doesn't need to work from a position of weakness. Scripture says that we have been received into a Kingdom that cannot be shaken (see Heb. 12:28). That Kingdom is intended to be the Kingdom of the unafraid. It is not a kingdom of poor souls struggling wearily down the path of fear and resignation—where the only relief is to die and go to heaven. Even though Satan uses fear as his primary weapon, the Scriptures tell us that we are in fact children of a Kingdom that has power to overcome the destructive forces of the evil one (see 2 Pet. 1:3; Eph.1:19).

As we develop a strong faith, we will diminish our fear. As we acquire a beautiful love, we will have nothing to fear. As we make a glorious hope, we ensure a future without fear.

CHAPTER 16

THE BIBLE AND INTERPERSONAL RELATIONSHIPS

We must, despite ourselves, turn heavenward our eyes.

—ALFRED DE MUSSET

How can a book that teaches interpersonal relationships neglect the Book that started it all? The Bible has the definitive approach to people's association with God and each other. If you really want to learn how to get along with people, then get into the Word. It's your best teacher and motivator. However, like a good sermon, *Sharpening Your People Skills* can illuminate biblical principles and help unlock truths that will smooth out relationships. If you want to get along with people, the first principle is:

BE THE BEST PERSON THAT YOU CAN BE

In the beginning God said, "Let us make man in our image, after our likeness" (Gen. 1:26). The first principle suggests that *if* we are in the image of God, we are contracted to be good, like God. Even more than good, we are intended to be perfect. That's why Jesus said, "Be ye therefore perfect, even as your Father which is in heaven is perfect" (Matt. 5:48). At least it is the original purpose and a high goal to stretch toward.

Good people get along with each other. The good even get along with the bad better than the bad do. In fact, bad people hate bad people with a purple passion. "When a man's ways please the Lord, he maketh even his enemies to be at peace with him" (Prov. 16:7).

When I worked at Terminal Island Federal Penitentiary as a psychologist, I observed that the convicts seldom formed friendly bonds with each other and frequently engaged in hateful slander. One day an inmate broke into the footlocker of another convict and stole some of his possessions. The man who had his possessions stolen ranted and raged and declared he would kill the man who stole from him. Ironically, the complainer had spent twenty-seven years of his life as a professional thief, breaking and entering, and stealing from thousands of people; yet, he declared, "I can't stand it when someone steals from me." The professional thief hated thieves, but he was friendly with honest men.

If you want to get along with people and have them treat you fairly, first of all, be a good honest person yourself. No one likes a thief much. Like the story of Judas, a thief usually doesn't turn out very well. Both the good and the bad prefer good people and will gravitate toward them.

DON'T BE ALONE, GET A COMPANION

The second principle from the Bible is found in Genesis 2:18, "The Lord God said, It is not good that the man should be alone; I will make him an help meet for him." If you want to be happy and get along with people, remember that everyone needs a companion, a friend, and a helper—someone to share the journey of life.

There is a lot of emphasis today on being your own person and doing your own thing, even to the extent of single parents raising children. It may be that we have no choice or can't find

a suitable companion, but who could possibly say that alone-
ness is better than togetherness. We were meant to be partners, not lone wolves. The rogue elephant usually storms
around in a very angry way.

People who have a significant other in their lives will automatically know how to get along better with strangers. Life is
meant to be lived in a partnership. Even the apostle Paul, who
had a call from God to be a bachelor, said, "Let every man
have his own wife, and let every woman have her own husband" (1 Cor. 7:2). God planned togetherness and taught it
from the very beginning. Of course, single people can have a
life. In fact, they probably will have trouble finding a mate if
they don't have a life. Often the companion of a single person
is a great cause; but the "two shall become one" concept
remains the best way to go, if possible.

There is another way of finding a companion. Jesus said,
"Where two or three are gathered together in my name, there
am I in the midst of them" (Matt. 18:20). He knew about
another type of togetherness. The perfect Son of God gathered
disciples around Him and established His church in deference
to the principle of God that we all need some significant associ-
ations. If you are having difficulty with people, don't run away
from them; run toward them and establish camaraderie, friendship, and close bonds.

The churches of the world are holding out their arms in a
passionate search to embrace people into the fellowship of the
kingdom. If you are having difficulty getting along with people,
go to church and find some good, empathetic friends. It is also
a quick and easy way to develop people skills.

ACCEPT PROBLEMS WITHOUT COMPLAINT

The next basic biblical principle of getting along with people
is found in Genesis 3:16–17 when God said to Eve, "I will
greatly increase your pains in childbearing" and to Adam,
"Cursed is the ground because of you, through painful toil you
will eat of it all the days of your life" (NIV). All of humankind

has been assigned problems, and it is important to accept our share with good grace, then we won't be so mean to people.

No one is free from pain or trouble. Anxiety, frustration, and fear are a normal part of life. I have my set of adversity, and so do my neighbors. We need to bear our troubles with good grace and help the people around us to bear theirs. In the Book of Acts we read the story of the apostle Paul who was whipped and thrown into the Philippian jail for preaching. The first thing he did was to sing songs of happiness. We also are to be "peculiar people" who "rejoice in the Lord always," even when unjustly treated.

The children of Israel wandered in the wilderness for forty years, mainly because they couldn't stop griping, complaining, and whining about every little thing.

I know a successful therapist whose first goal in therapy is to get people to stop singing a version of "The Whiffenpuff Song": "I'm a poor lost sheep, who can't get his own way. Whine. Whine. Whine." When people learn to stop whining, they get well.

Because of our sins and as a test of our faith, God Himself has given us our share of troubles. Receive your part as if they were your test and your challenge. You are not alone, everyone has his share—some much worse than you. If you can accept this principle, you will have gone a long way toward living comfortably with and understanding people.

YOU *ARE* YOUR BROTHER'S KEEPER

The next basic truth is found in the fourth chapter of Genesis, verses 9 and 10. Cain had just murdered his brother, Abel, and God asked Cain, "Where is your brother Abel?"

"I don't know," he replied. "Am I my brother's keeper?"

"The LORD said, 'What have you done? Listen. Your brother's blood cries out to me from the ground'" (NIV). Then God punished Cain.

Cain had thrown a hot potato at God, and God tossed it right back and set a standard for us all. If we become aware of this rule of human conduct dictated by God, "You *are* your brother's keeper," then we will truly know how to get along with people. We are responsible for what happens to people; therefore, we must do all we can to do good, not evil.

Jesus said it a little more succinctly: "Love your neighbor as yourself" (Matt. 19:19); and, "All things whatsoever you would that men should do unto you, even so do you also unto them" (Matt. 7:12).

What goes around, comes around. "If you bite and devour one another," you will be consumed by one another (see Gal. 5:15). Twenty-five thousand men are confined in California prisons because they have molested children. Other felons frequently assault these men using the rationalization, "If they assault little helpless children, we will assault them." Yes, we are our brother's keeper, and if we hurt people, we will get hurt. Conversely, if we help people, we will receive help.

ESTABLISH STRONG FAMILY BONDS

The next standard of interpersonal behavior is found in Genesis 7:1, where the Lord said to Noah, "Go into the ark, you and your whole family, because I have found you righteous in this generation." As far as we know, Noah was actually the righteous one, but God knew a man must have his family with him, so the whole family went into the ark. The principle of relationship is simple. The family is the basic unit of civilization.

When people don't get along in the home, they probably won't get along in the street. The Ten Commandments tells us, "Honor thy father and thy mother that thy days may be long upon the land which the LORD thy God giveth thee" (Exod. 20:12).

A few years ago, the media reported that thousands of abandoned children roamed the streets in Rio de Janeiro, Brazil. Only 40 percent of them ever reached adulthood— and 75 percent of those were severely impaired. We need our families to survive.

I have given thousands of psychometric tests to disturbed people. Eighty percent of these mentally or even criminally ill people come from fractured, dysfunctional families. It is very rare to find a convict in prison who comes from a home with a loving mother and father. The involvement of the home provides the best answer to the rising tide of delinquency and deteriorating values. We just can't get along with people if we can't get along in our families. One of the best bets in learning how to establish good relationships is to establish a good home. The strong family, bonded together under God, ensures people skills that will long endure.

INCLUDE GOD IN YOUR PLANS

In the eleventh chapter of Genesis, we read that all the world spoke one language. They decided to build a tower to heaven to glorify themselves. They did not consult God, nor did they honor Him in any way. So God came down and confounded their language and scattered them across the face of the earth. All these people were getting along with each other, but they left out God and soon they didn't understand each other, undoubtedly fought bitterly, despised each other, and fled from each other's presence. All because they left out God.

The Book of James warns us not to say that we have any plans for today or tomorrow, but rather to say, "If it is the Lord's will, we will live and do this or that" (James 4:15, NIV). When we include God in our plans, how can we help but get along better with people?

How can we possibly get along with each other if we exclude the Heavenly Father from our family, our plans, and our lives. Jesus said, "Seek ye first the kingdom of God, and his righteousness; and all these things will be added unto you" (Matt. 6:33). We are to put God first. Exodus 20:3 exhorts us, "Thou shalt have no other gods before me." Jesus said that we are to love the Lord our God with all our heart, with all our soul, with all our mind, and with all our strength (see Luke 10:27). Did you ever hear of loving someone like that and then excluding them? No! It can't be done!

CHOOSE FULFILLING WORK

Genesis 2:15 reads, "The LORD God took the man and put him in the Garden of Eden to work it and take care of it" (NIV). From the very beginning God intended man and woman to work. God also brought the animals to man to see what he would name them, and whatever he named them, that was it. People were intended to name things (the first step of the scientific method), do work projects, and even replenish the earth. One commentary says that *replenish* means to fix things. OK, if you want to get along with people, get back to basics: repair things, build, and work.

One time I was out of work for a year. I couldn't get along with myself, my beautiful wife, my lovely children, my mother, my friends, or anyone I loved, and I was very nasty to the people on the freeway. The day I got a job, it all changed. Work normalized my relationships.

To me, the worst thing we can do with our prison population is to let them hang around, watch television, lift weights, and swap stories. I advocate putting them to work. I don't mean sweatshops, but I do mean work. In fact, I don't hate anyone enough to give them a life of ease. Even old retired men like me need to pound away at the computer every day. Just lying around will kill a person faster than anything I know. Jesus said, "I have glorified thee on earth: I have finished the work which thou gavest me to do" (John 17:4).

We can't glorify God, nor can we get along with people, unless we work.

LEARN HOW TO SAY NO

Way back in the beginning God told Adam and Eve that they could eat of every fruit of the Garden, except one. It was *yes* to everything except a *no* to just one. You know the story: they didn't honor the *no*, so God took away a lot of the *yeses*. It's still true.

A *yes* is meaningless if not backed up by a powerful *no*. What woman or man wants a husband or wife who says yes to everyone. We want them to say yes to us and no to everyone else. Yes to everyone makes that special yes to us meaningless.

When Ronald Reagan was president of the United States, his wife, Nancy, sponsored an antidrug campaign with the words, "Just say no." If we try to please people and make them like us by saying yes to everything, we will be heartily despised, avoided, and even hated. Principles and standards are universally accepted, admired, and a necessary part of valid human relationships. We disrespect people who say yes, yes, yes to every request. They do not win admiration, but rather revulsion.

In order to say no politely with a minimum of offense, we need to:

1. Speak calmly. When we use too much force, anger, or emotional power, we set the other person to resist.

2. Don't elaborate. The more excuses we use, the weaker the no. Explanations will bring an effort on the other person's part to persuade us.

3. Don't argue. You are liable to lose. If you have said no and the persuader tries to convince you, walk away or at least delay your decision.

4. Don't take offense. The more emotional anger you put into your no the more likely you are to change. Often emotions overrule intellect.

5. Don't let yourself feel guilty. A no is a no, and you have a right to say it.

6. Remember your moral codes. The more you keep them, the stronger they get. The more you break them, the weaker they get.

7. Prepare to set your resolve to say no.

   (a) Associate with good people.
   (b) Keep yourself healthy and strong.
   (c) Attend church and read your Bible.
   (d) Do good for people. That will minimize the bad.
   (e) Set some worthwhile goals.

MAKE FRIENDS,
EVEN WITH YOUR ENEMIES

"Woe unto you, when all men shall speak well of you! for so did their fathers to the false prophets. But I say unto you which hear, Love your enemies, do good to them which hate you, Bless them that curse you, and pray for them which despitefully use you" (Luke 6:26–28).

Most of the great men in the Bible had enemies, including Jesus. He said, "If they have called the master of the house Beelzebub, how much more shall they call them of his household?" (Matt. 10:25). Which one of the prophets did they not stone or draw and quarter? Obviously, John the Baptist didn't get along with Herod's wife very well. She had him decapitated for his remarks. It probably teaches us that if you are going to be a prophet, you will have to pay the price.

Jesus said, "Blessed are they which are persecuted for righteousness sake" (Matt. 5:10). If people are going to be your enemy, let it be because you are right, not wrong. If we are wrong or do harm to people and they become our enemies, we must repent, confess our sin, make restitution if possible, and change our behavior. If we do good to people and they become our enemies, we must pray for them. God will be dealing with them.

David had lots of enemies, but he declared, "Thou preparest a table before me in the presence of my enemies" (Ps. 23:5). We must know that God will richly bless us if we are righteous in the presence of our enemies.

The apostle Paul had so many enemies that we sometimes forget how many friends he had. People in the church came to visit him whenever he was imprisoned, and on every missionary journey, crowds of people came to hear him.

However, the following stories illustrate another basic teaching concerning enemies:

Jacob came back home to his father's house after a twenty-year odyssey. Esau came out to meet him with four hundred heavily armed men. Jacob had stolen the birthright and the blessing of Esau, and now he was rightly fearful that Esau was his enemy. So in Genesis 32 and 33 we read how Jacob tried to appease Esau by gifts of livestock. Jacob also wrestled with an angel of God for protection, and when he met Esau he bowed down to the earth seven times. Of course, "Esau ran to meet him, and embraced him, and fell on his neck, and kissed him: and they wept" (Gen. 33:4). Jacob turned a mortal enemy into a friend.

When David was on his way to kill Nabal, who had refused to give food for his men after David had protected his flocks, Nabal's wife, Abigail, quickly brought gifts to David to win his favor. Jesus said, "Settle matters quickly with your adversary who is taking you to court" (Matt. 5:25, NIV). If you can, make friends of your enemies, lest they mow you down.

HAVE FAITH IN GOD

The Bible asks the question, "If someone says, 'I love God,' and hates his brother, . . . whom he has seen, how can he love God whom he has not seen?" (1 John 4:20, NKJV). By analogy we can say, "How can we say we have faith in God whom we have not seen, if we don't have faith in our neighbor whom we have seen?" And the answer is: We can't. Without faith it is impossible to be well-pleasing unto God, and that applies to people also.

Faith in God means faith in what He has created, how He did it, and even why. People are said to be created in the image of God, and hence His greatest creation. Faith in God automatically includes faith in people. When we lose faith in people, we lose the ability to deal with them, and we short-change our belief in God.

We often confuse faith and facts. A fact does not need faith, it is already true. Faith is an optimistic look at the future. The fact may be that we are in prison, chained to the wall; our faith in God and people makes us sing songs of joy and break down prison walls. The fact may be that we are paralyzed and dying with a stroke; but our faith lifts up our hearts in the midst of adversity, turns off the bitterness, and enables us to live with people with a sweetness that belies our condition.

Freida Mae Clayville had leukemia and bled through her pores and suffered great pain. Ministers came from miles around to visit her in the Boise County Hospital, not to commiserate, but to exult in the joyous way she read the Bible and the happy spirit she expressed to people. She died, but her faith in God and people encouraged happy relationships here and throughout eternity.

When we have faith in God, we will have hope for the future, and we will be today's most agreeable person.

Follow the Teachings of Jesus

Jesus was a master of people skills because He knew what was in people, and how they were made (see John 2:24–25). He offended the Pharisees because they were hypocritical and misused their power, but the common people heard Him gladly, and thousands of people were blessed by His teaching and His healing. Since that time, millions of people have fallen in love with the winsome Son of God.

"And there are also many other things that Jesus did, the which, if they should be written everyone, I suppose that even the world itself could not contain the books that should be written" (John 21:25). So, who am I to condense the teaching of Jesus on just a few pages? But I at least must share my intrigue of the final sermon that Jesus preached to His disciples as He was sitting on the Mount of Olives, just before His crucifixion. Jesus wished to fulfill the promise of the angels at His birth, "Peace on earth, goodwill toward men." In His final sermon (Matt. 24–25) He taught these four ideas:

Expect the Second Coming of Christ

"Keep watch, because you do not know on what day your Lord will come" (Matt. 24:42, NIV).

What has this got to do with people skills? Much in every way. The person expecting the second coming of Christ, looking for the new heaven and earth, counting on the rapture, hoping for eternal life, will not be crotchety and mean to his neighbor. In fact, you will not need to teach him much about how to grease the slide of interpersonal relationships; he will be good to people because God has been and will be good to him. He says, "Eternity, thou pleasing thought." With that faith, what on earth can get us down?

KEEP GOING TO THE END

"The wise, however, took oil in jars along with their lamps" (Matt. 25:4, NIV).

The whole Sermon on the Mount emphasizes the theme "Keep watch, because you do not know the day or the hour." However, each point in the sermon has a different twist, and each one teaches us how to get along with people. So, what's this keeping oil in lamps?

Jesus had said in one of His first sermons, "Let your light shine before men that they may see your good works and glorify your Father which is in heaven" (Matt. 5:16). In other words, don't hide your goodness, don't hide your personality (have salt in yourself), and supply yourself with plenty of oil so that your goodness won't run out at the end of your days. "He that endureth to the end shall be saved" (Matt. 10:22).

E. Stanley Jones, a Methodist missionary to India, wrote his final book entitled *The Divine Yes* when he was eighty-seven years old and paralyzed from a stroke. In this book he declared that he was going to maintain his Christian attitude, in spite of all his trouble. It was the final test: when he said yes to God till the end, he knew God would say yes to him through eternity.

INCREASE WHAT YOU HAVE

"For unto every one that hath shall be given, and he shall have abundance; but from him that hath not shall be taken away even that which he hath" (Matt. 25:29).

Be a good steward of your money and talents. Money is the root of all kinds of evil and we are not to trust in it—we are to trust in God. In fact, "it is easier for a camel to go through the eye of a needle than for a rich man to enter the kingdom of God" (Matt. 19:24, NIV). However, there is another side. Jesus said that we are to be good stewards of our money, possessions, and talents. In fact, if we don't make our money and talents grow, they may be taken away from us.

So, what does this have to do with getting along with people? If you don't have anything and you haven't done anything with your life, God won't bless you and people won't like you.

I know a number of people who have a modest amount of wealth. One man said to me, "When I was poor, I always picked up the check at restaurants. Now that I am rich, people fight to pick up the check for me." Sure enough, I picked up the check. The old saying,"The rich get richer and the poor get poorer," is true. In order to have friends and influence, we must have something, be able to do something, or be rich in wisdom. Blank people are avoided.

HELP PEOPLE

"Inasmuch as you did not do it to one of the least of these, you did not do it to Me" (Matt. 25:45, NKJV).

In His final sermon Jesus said, "Come, you who are blessed by my Father; take your inheritance, the kingdom prepared for you since the creation of the world. For I was hungry and you gave me something to eat, I was thirsty and you gave me something to drink, I was a stranger and you invited me in, I needed clothes and you clothed me, I was sick and you looked after me, I was in prison and you came to visit me" (Matt. 25:34–36, NIV). Jesus taught us to help people.

Every now and then I counsel with a person who has adopted a frantic, hysterical response to life. They frequently overinterpret every little thing and often become very unhappy and extremely paranoid in dealing with people. A popular approach to therapy is to get these people to believe that they are responding to some terrible repressed memory. I think along more simple lines—the hysterics are too involved with themselves. They need to be involved in helping people, just as Jesus said and did. When we help people, we have almost mastered the art of people skills.

IN A NUTSHELL

- Be the best person you can be.
- Don't be alone, get a companion.
- Accept problems without complaint.
- Know you are your brother's keeper.
- Establish strong family bonds.
- Include God in your plans.
- Choose fulfilling work.
- Learn how to say no.
- Make friends, even with your enemies.
- Have faith in God.
- Follow the teachings of Jesus.
    1. Expect the second coming of Christ.
    2. Keep going to the end; don't give up.
    3. Increase what you have.
    4. Help people.

CONCLUSION

The book *Sharpening Your People Skills* builds on some foundation principles of human personality and relationships that have been known for thousands of years.

About five hundred years before the birth of Christ, a Greek historian named Herodotus told the story of the Cimmerian race. The Cimmerians lived in the southern part of the country we today call Iran. North of them, next to the Caspian Sea in Russia, lived the Scythians. They wore goblets made of skulls on their belts like our Marines wear grenades. They were drunken, savage people. When the Scythians got restless and made motions as if to invade Cimmeria, the Cimmerians got frightened and called a counsel of their whole nation. One half of the Cimmerians, the Royal tribe, advised fighting the Scythians to the bitter end. The other half, the Natives, declared that the Scythians were a superior force. They determined to retire without a blow and yield their lands to the invaders. The Natives and the Royals argued their points so vigorously that they got into a fierce fight.

In a battle to the death, the Natives killed off all the Royals. Of course, the Scythians heard about the war and viciously invaded, destroying the Cimmerian castles, the ferry transportation system, the houses, the cities, and all evidence of the Cimmerian civilization. They made bond slaves of all women. They cannibalized some and killed by torture the rest of the Native men and children.

Herodotus told this story in his fourth book entitled *Melpomeme*, and he fixed a moral to it that still applies today. "The enemy can destroy the family, clan, or nation that fights among themselves." The Bible puts it, "If you bite and devour one another, beware lest you be consumed by one another" (Gal. 5:15, NKJV).

1. *People skills begin with those who live in our environment.* It will do very little good to sharpen our people skills if we do not apply the principles to ourselves, our friends, our family, and community. Personal conflicts, in-fighting, and civil war all destroy the ability to cope with others. If we truly sharpen our people skills, we must begin at home.

2. In order to get along with people, we must be convinced of the necessity to do it. *We must take time to learn the rules and practice them, and bend our wills to the discipline of successful interpersonal relationships.* If a person is not convinced that people skills are necessary, he will be exterminated in the "southern plains of Iran" and never be heard of again!

3. *In a kind way, tell people the truth.* In the long run, nothing works but the truth. When I was a little boy, my mother taught me to tell the truth, but it took years to learn how to do it in a kind way. A soft voice, euphemisms, a friendly approach, and caring for people will help us to "speak the truth in love" (Eph. 4:15).

4. *Treat people as you want to be treated.* Sometimes crooks or people who are mentally ill want to be treated in a sadistic way, but most of us have high standards on how we

want the Golden Rule applied to our situation. So, you want people to treat you with tolerance and forgiveness; then do it, and it will be done to you.

5. *Learn the rules and keep the customs.* A missionary friend of mine was kicked out of an African village because he violated the formalities of village life. They could not receive his gospel if he could not adjust to their ways.

6. *Control your temper.* Anger and hostility seldom breeds anything but terror, reciprocal anger, and war. Carefully control your anger, and it can be a great motivational force, but the minute it spills over the banks, destruction visits the land.

7. *Help people, don't just take.* Since the beginning, we have been under the admonition to be our brother's keeper, to bear one another's burdens, to assist our neighbor, and be hospitable. It's easy to win friends when we are helpful. The Word speaks, "Give, and it shall be given unto you" (Luke 6:38).

8. *Be careful of your verbalizations.* Don't offend people with your words. We often react to words as if they were alive. Words heal and activate, so use them to build up and not tear down.

9. *Be positive; encourage rather than criticize.* Make an attempt to lift people up and make them feel good. To judge, criticize, and complain creates anger and depression; furthermore, it probably doesn't change anyone. Tell people what they are doing right, and they will be inclined to repeat it.

10. *Listen with your third ear.* That means to listen very carefully and pick up the true meaning behind careless, vindictive words. Not everyone saying they hate us really does. Be intuitive and listen for the truth. Understand people at a deep level.

11. *Be happy, upbeat, and enthusiastic.* Personality has certain genetic tendencies, but happiness and enthusiasm are a

choice. One personality building course had for it's motto: "Act enthusiastic, and you'll be enthusiastic."

12. *Start all relationships, even confrontations, in a friendly way.* You may end up quarreling (hopefully not), but you don't have to start that way. Be nice, be kind, be gentle, and be friendly; you will have a much better chance of ending the same way.

13. *Don't bear grudges or take vengeance.* "Vengeance is Mine, I will repay, says the Lord" (Rom. 12:19, NKJV). More murders and injustice has been committed in the name of envy, grudges, and vengeance than any other condition. Even today there is no peace in the Holy Land because of the principle of vengeance. Forgive, and you will be forgiven. Take vengeance, and it will be taken on you—forever, a vicious circle.

14. *Choose to love life, your neighbors, your circumstances, and yourself.* Put most of your attention into the things you love, and minimize the things you hate. Love everyone, even your enemies, and you will be blessed full measure. Love never fails, and it is the keystone of *Sharpening Your People Skills*.